SHAMBHALA DRAGON EDITIONS

The dragon is an age-old symbol of the highest spiritual essence, embodying wisdom, strength, and the divine power of transformation. In this spirit, Shambhala Dragon Editions offers a treasury of readings in the sacred knowledge of Asia. In presenting the works of authors both ancient and modern, we seek to make these teachings accessible to lovers of wisdom everywhere.

Glimpses of Abhidharma

From a Seminar on Buddhist Psychology

Chögyam Trungpa

Shambhala
Boston & London
2001

Shambhala Publications, Inc.
Horticultural Hall
300 Massachusetts Avenue
Boston, Massachusetts 02115
www.shambhala.com

Printed in the United States of America
Distributed in the United States by Random House
and in Canada by Random House of Canada Ltd

*The Library of Congress catalogues the previous edition
of this book as follows:*
Trungpa, Chögyam, 1939–1987
Glimpses of Abhidharma.
(Shambhala Dragon)
Originally published: Boulder, Colo.:
Prajña Press, 1978, c1975.
1. Abhidharma. 2. Buddhism—Psychology.
I. Title
BQ4195.T78   1987   150.19'0882943   86-31409
ISBN 0-87773-282-5 (pbk.)
ISBN 1-57062-764-9 (pbk.)

BVG 01

CONTENTS

Introduction   1

Form   9

Feeling   21

Perception   31

Intellect   47

Meditation   65

Consciousness   73

Auspicious Coincidence   91

Practice and Intellect   107

GLIMPSES OF ABHIDHARMA

INTRODUCTION

T HE ABHIDHARMA is perhaps regarded as dry and scholarly, theoretical. We will see. In any case I would like to welcome those of you who are brave and willing to go into it. To a certain extent you are warriors.

I have decided to present the abhidharma because I feel it is necessary in studying the Buddhist tradition to start from scratch, to begin at the beginning and present the pure, immaculate, genuine teaching. We have been doing that so far in terms of the practice of meditation and in terms of the theoretical understanding of the teaching as well. I feel it is important that the teachings be presented that way. The presentation of Eastern teachings in the West has been particularly haphazard. The teachers have something to say and they say it, but perhaps it does not reach the audience effectively, in such a way as to create the right situation for practice. These teachers have been trained and have practiced and received transmission in their own countries, but that was a different cultural situation in which a certain environment of discipline was taken for granted. They seem to presume that the same cultural background also exists in the West. But perhaps that is not the case. So for us in the West to get into a spiritual teaching, we have to get into the basic core of it. We have to build a really good foundation before we get into practices such as the yoga of inner heat or start levitating or whatever.

In getting back to the basic principles, there could be two approaches. Some people feel inclined to work purely on the intuitive or emotional level; others feel that approach is not

1

fundamental enough and want to work on the scholarly or theoretical aspect. I would not say that these two ways conflict, but
rather that they are two channels through which to approach the
subject. What we are trying to do here is to neglect neither the
intellect nor the intuition, but to combine the two together. A real
understanding of the teachings must be an intelligent one and a
human one at the same time. The intelligent aspect is the theory;
the human side is the intuitive, personal feeling of the teaching
and the learning process involved in it. One might say that the
study of the abhidharma is a theoretical one in some sense; but it
also has the quality of personality, individuality, because the
abhidharma is a survey of the psychology of the human mind. It is
part of the basic philosophy of Buddhism, common to all
schools—the Theravadins, the Tibetans and so on.

The abhidharma is part of what is called the *tripitaka*, the
"three baskets" or "three heaps." These are the three bodies of
teaching that constitute the Buddhist scriptures. The first is
called the *vinayapitaka*, which is concerned with discipline, the
practicalities of how to live one's life in the world and understand
it at the same time. The *vinaya* is presented in such a way that
there is no conflict between understanding and practical discipline. The second "basket" is the *sutrapitaka* which deals with
certain meditative practices and various ways of training the
mind, ways of accepting and using both intellect and intuition as
supports of meditation. The third is the *abhidharmapitaka*. Having seen the practical aspect of how you relate to the world and
also the meditative, psychological aspect, we now begin to work
on the background of the whole thing. This is almost, one might
say, preparation to teach. The abhidharma in a sense tells us how,
having understood everything, to communicate with others.

Many modern psychologists have found that the discoveries
and explanations of the abhidharma coincide with their own
recent discoveries and new ideas; as though the abhidharma,
which was taught 2,500 years ago, had been redeveloped in the
modern idiom.

Introduction

The abhidharma deals with the five skandhas. The skandhas represent the constant structure of human psychology as well as its pattern of evolution and the pattern of evolution of the world. The skandhas are also related to blockages of different types— spiritual ones, material ones, emotional ones. An understanding of the five skandhas shows that once we are tuned into the basic core of egohood, then anything—any experience, any inspiration—can be made into a further blockage or can become a way of freeing ourselves. Abhidharma is a very precise way of looking at mind. Any tendency of mind, even the subtlest suggestion of a tendency can be viewed with great precision—even something as slight as the irritation from having a fly perched on one's leg. That irritation, for example, might be classified as a friendly one which merely tends to frighten the fly away or an aggressive one which moves to kill it.

The abhidharma deals very precisely and impartially with our particular type of mind and it is tremendously helpful for us to see our mind that way. This does not mean being purely scholarly and intellectual. We can relate to little irritations like the one of the fly as just the sort of happening that makes up the human situation. We do not particularly make a big deal about it, but we see it precisely. This eventually becomes very helpful. It is helpful not only for pure meditation but also meditation in action. The whole approach of Buddhism is oriented towards dealing with everyday life situations rather than just meditating in order to attain enlightenment. Throughout the three *pitakas* there is very little emphasis on enlightenment. The *pitakas* are handbooks of how to live in terms of the awakened state of mind, but very much on the kitchen-sink level. They are concerned with how to step out of our usual sleepwalking and deal really with actual situations. The abhidharma is a very important part of that general instruction.

Our particular study here of the abhidharma, because of limitations of time and space and the patience of the audience, has to be something of a rough survey. Nevertheless, as a basic introduction, I think it will be extremely useful.

Question. I didn't really understand the difference between the *sutrapitaka* and the *abhidharmapitaka.*

Rinpoche. The *sutrapitaka* gives the techniques of meditation while the abhidharma describes the accomplished experience of meditation so that you can relate with other people about it, as well as yourself. Rather than being a cookbook, it presumes that you are familiar with certain ideas and experiences and proceeds to formulate them with great precision. That is why recent translators have run into difficulty with Buddhist texts—they have not had experience of what is being talked about. That is what is lacking in a lot of the translations.

Question. What does *abhidharma* mean?

Rinpoche. The Tibetan for *abhidharma* is *chö ngönpa* [chos mngon.pa]. *Chö* means *dharma* in Sanskrit, the law or "isness" of things. *Ngönpa* refers to something visible or apparent, something available visually. It means, almost, something which is predictable, something you can interpret or see the pattern of. So you could say *abhidharma* means the "pattern of the dharma." Here "dharma" could be the dharma of cooking, the dharma of driving a motorcar, any kind of dharma—not dharma with a capital "d" particularly. It is the intimate, homey quality of the dharma which is very vividly presented in the abhidharma.

Question. I heard that in certain Buddhist countries that stress the study of the abhidharma the practice of meditation fell away. Is there a kind of danger in the *abhidharmapitaka* teachings, that if one uses them in the wrong way to relate to kitchen-sink problems, it might lead one to think one could do without meditation?

Rinpoche. I think that is highly possible, definitely. That is a problem that has come up; and in fact it is a main cause of the degeneration of the buddhadharma in the whole Buddhist world. I have heard that an outstanding scholar from Ceylon has said that no one has attained enlightenment in the last 500 years, but that nevertheless it is our duty to keep all the theories alive so that maybe one day somebody will click. Actually, it is a basic idea among Buddhist scholars who emphasize mainly the scholarly side of the teaching that it is dangerous to begin meditating before you have mastered the theory. Then, once you have discovered everything intellectually, how to do it, what the idea is behind it, once you have gone through all the psychological images intellectually, then you do not really have to meditate because you know it all already. That approach goes along with the idea of Buddha as superscholar. Since the idea of awakened mind or enlightenment exists in the tradition, these scholars must have some view of it. They have no way of interpreting it other than as knowing everything. They think that if someone has ten or twelve Ph.D.'s, he will probably attain enlightenment because he has all the answers. Then someone with one Ph.D. should have attained partial enlightenment, but as we know this does not happen at all. So being a superscholar is not the answer.

The contemplative traditions of Buddhism, such as the Tibetan and Zen traditions, emphasize practice very strongly and see study as something that should go side by side with it. Here the idea of learning is that it is a process of new discovery, new scientific discovery, which is actual experience. There is a tremendous difference between putting something under a microscope, actually seeing it with your own eyes, and just purely analyzing the topic. Anything can be analyzed, but if you have no experience of it there is no basis for analysis. So the idea in the contemplative tradition is that one should have some basic training in meditation practice, however primitive it may be, and then begin to work on the intellectual aspect. This way the teaching is treated as a confirmation of experience rather than purely as a bank of information.

Question. Could you explain this tendency in us to be satisfied with theory instead of being freer and more open in terms of actual experience?

Rinpoche. I suppose the main tendency might be the tendency to make secure what we are doing. You see, on the whole practice is a sloppy job. You have to accept that you have been a fool and start with being foolish. For instance, in the beginning deciding to try the practice of meditation is just leaping to some conclusion about what to do. And even in doing the practice at the beginning, rather than really meditating you just imagine you are meditating. So to begin with, the whole thing is based on confusion and confusion is accepted as part of the path. And since the situation is very loose and unorganized, it is as though you are leaping into unknown territory. A lot of people find that very frightening. You are not quite sure what you are involved with. But that is the only way to get into the practice. Being a fool then becomes a stepping-stone. The foolishness wears itself out and the thing behind the foolishness begins to peep through. It is like wearing out a shoe—your genuine feet begin to appear from behind your shoe.

You see there is a tremendous amount of fear involved and so a certain amount of security is needed. This particular answer does not answer all your questions of security. It does not really promise anything, it just pushes you overboard. It points out the situation of needing security and being frightened of that situation. Once we step out of that concern for security and are willing to be raw and rugged, personal, as we are, somehow a certain relaxation takes place. We discover that the more we let go the more comes back to us, rather than that we lose our grip on anything. Then a real relationship to your situation begins to develop.

Introduction

The great problem is that spiritual teachings have been used as a way of securing ourselves, gaining a higher level of stability in terms of ego. This is our inevitable starting point. We cannot ignore this or push it away. We must start with the mistakes and that is always a problem. There is the fear and need for security that makes acceptance of spontaneity extremely difficult. As it says in the *Dhammapada*, "He who knows he's a fool is a wise man indeed."

FORM

WE COULD BEGIN by discussing the origin of all psychological problems, the origin of neurotic mind. This is a tendency to identify oneself with desires and conflicts related to a world outside. And the question is immediately there as to whether such conflicts actually exist externally or whether they are internal. This uncertainty solidifies the whole sense that a problem of some kind exists. What is real? What is not real? That is always our biggest problem. It is ego's problem.

The abhidharma, its whole contents with all the details, is based on the point of view of egolessness. When we talk about egolessness, that does not mean simply the absence of ego itself. It means also the absence of the projections of ego. Egolessness comes more or less as a by-product of seeing the transitory, transparent nature of the world outside. Once we have dealt with the projections of ego and seen their transitory and transparent nature, then ego has no reference point, nothing to relate to. So the notions of inside and outside are interdependent—ego began and its projections began. Ego managed to maintain its identity by means of its projections. When we are able to see the projections as nonsubstantial, ego becomes transparent correspondingly.

According to the abhidharma, ego consists, in one of its aspects, of eight kinds of consciousness. There are the six sense consciousnesses (thinking mind is regarded as a sixth sense). Then there is a seventh consciousness, which has the nature of ignorance, cloudiness, confusion. This cloudy mind is an overall structure which runs right through the six sense consciousnesses.

9

Each sense consciousness relates to this cloudy situation of not knowing exactly what you are doing. The seventh consciousness is an absence of precision. It is very blind.

The eighth consciousness is what you could call the common ground or the unconscious ground of all this. It is the ground that makes it possible for all the other seven to operate. This ground is different from the basic ground of which I have sometimes spoken, which is the background of all of existence and contains samsara and nirvana both. The eighth consciousness is not as basic as that ground. It is a kind of secondary basic level where confusion has already begun; and that confusion provides an accommodation for the other seven consciousnesses to operate.

There is an evolutionary process which starts from this unconscious ground, the eighth consciousness. The cloudy consciousness arises from that and then the six sense consciousnesses. Even the six senses evolve in a certain order according to the level of experiential intensity of each of them. The most intense level is attained with sight which develops last.

These eight types of consciousness can be looked at as being on the level of the first of the five skandhas, form. They are the form of ego, the tangible aspect of it. They constitute the ultimate grounding element of ego—as far as ego's grounding goes; which is not very far. Still, from a relative point of view, they do comprise something fixed, something definite.

I think to place this in perspective, it would be good to discuss briefly the basic ground—even though the abhidharma teaching does not talk very much about it—the all-prevading basic ground which we have just contrasted to the eighth consciousness. This basic ground does not depend on relative situations at all. It is natural being which just is. Energies appear out of this basic ground and those energies are the source of the development of relative situations. Sparks of duality, intensity and sharpness, flashes of wisdom and knowledge—all sorts of things come out of the basic ground. So the basic ground is the source of confusion and also the source of liberation. Both liberation and confusion are that energy which happens constantly, which sparks out and then goes back to its basic nature, like clouds (as Milarepa described it) emerging from and disappearing back into the sky.

As for ego's type of ground, the eighth consciousness, that arises when the energy which flashes out of the basic ground brings about a sort of blinding effect, bewilderment. That bewilderment becomes the eighth consciousness, the basic ground for ego. Dr. Guenther calls it "bewilderment-errancy." It is error that comes out of being bewildered—a kind of panic. If the energy were to go along with its own process of speed, there would be no panic. It is like driving a car fast; if you go along with the speed, you are able to maneuver accordingly. But if you suddenly panic with the thought that you have been going too fast without realizing it, you jam on the brakes and probably have an accident. Something suddenly freezes and brings the bewilderment of not knowing how to conduct the situation. Then actually the situation takes you over. Rather than just being completely one with the projection, the projection takes you over. Then the unexpected power of the projection comes back to you as your own doing, which creates extremely powerful and impressive bewilderment. That bewilderment acts as the basic ground, the secondary basic ground of ego, away from the primordial basic ground.

So ego is the ultimate relative, the source of all the relative concepts in the whole samsaric world. You cannot have criteria, notions of comparison, without ego. Things begin from ego's impression of relativity. Even nirvana begins that way. When ego began, nirvana, the other side of the same coin, began also. Without ego, there could be no such thing as nirvana or liberation, since a free state without relativity would be the case. So as ego develops, freedom and imprisonment begin to exist; and that relative situation contains the basic quality of ignorance.

The abhidharma does not talk very much about ignorance in the fundamental sense of ignoring oneself, but understanding this adds a further dimension to the teaching of the eight consciousnesses. Once there is bewilderment, then a sort of doubletake begins to happen of wanting to find out where you were, what you are, where you are at. But the nature of the bewilderment is that you do not want to go back and find out your original situation, you do not want to undo everything and go back. Since, with the bewilderment, you have created something to latch onto, you want to ignore the case history that led to that altogether. You want to make the best of the present moment and cling to it. That is the ignoring—refusing to go back because it is too painful, too frightening. As they say, "ignorance is bliss." Ignoring of ignoring is bliss, as least from ego's point of view.

This understanding of ignorance comes from the mahamudra teaching of the vajrayana tradition. The difference between the abhidharma and basic sutra teachings on ignorance and the more direct and daring mahamudra teaching is that the sutra and abhidharma teaching relates to ignorance as a one-way process—bewilderment and grasping and the six sense consciousnesses develop and ignorance takes over. But in the vajrayana teaching, ignorance is seen not only from the angle of the development of ego, but also as containing the potential for wisdom. This is not mentioned at all in the lower teachings. But within the eight consciousnesses, including the six sense consciousnesses, there actually is the possibility of ignorance turning into wisdom. This is a key point because wisdom cannot be born from theory, it must be born from your actual state of mind which is the working basis for all spiritual practice.

The wisdom of dealing with situations as they are, and that is what wisdom is, contains tremendous precision that could not come from anywhere else but the physical situations of sight, smell, feelings, touchable objects, and sounds. The earthy situation of actual things as they are is the source of wisdom. You can become completely one with smell, with sight, with sound, and your knowledge *about* them ceases to exist; your knowledge becomes wisdom. There is nothing to know about things as an external educational process. You become completely one with them; complete absorption takes place with sounds, smells, sights and so on. This approach is at the core of the mandala principle of the vajrayana teaching. At the same time, the great importance given to the six sense consciousnesses in the abhidharma has a similar concrete significance in its application to the practice of meditation and a person's way of relating to his experiences. Both levels of teaching put tremendous emphasis on direct relationship with the down-to-earth aspect of experience.

Question. Can you say more about how the six senses connect up with meditation?

Rinpoche. The implication of the abhidharma teaching on the six senses for the practice of meditation is identifying yourself with sounds, touchable objects, feelings, breathing and so on. The only way to develop sound meditative technique is to take something ordinary and use that. Unless you take something simple, the whole state of mind of your meditation will be based on the conflict of what is real and what is not and your relationship to that. This brings all kinds of complications and one begins to interpret these complications as psychological problems, neurotic problems, and to develop a sort of paranoid frame of mind in which what is going on represents to one much more than is actually there. So the whole idea is to start by relating to nonduality on a practical level, to step out of these paranoid conflicts of who in us is controlling who. We should just get into actual things, sights and sounds as they are. A basic part of the tradition of meditation is using the sense perceptions as a way of relating with the earth. They are sort of middlemen for dealing with the earth. They contain neither good nor bad, are connected with neither spirituality nor samsara, nor anything at all. They are just neutral.

Question. Ignorance seems to take on different values at different times, if I understand you. Could you explain that further?

Rinpoche. Ignorance is an evolutionary process. It does not just happen as one bulk, so to speak, but develops and grows like a plant. You have a seed and then manure; then the plant grows and finally blossoms. As we have said, the beginning of that ignorance is bewilderment, panic. It is the ultimate panic, which does not even contain fear. Being just pure panic, it transcends fear. It is something very meditative in that sense, almost spiritual—a spiritual absorption. It is that profound; it comes right from the depths of your very being. That ignorance is the seed of what you are. It is fundamental, neutral, without any concepts or ideas of any kind. Just pure panic, one hundred percent panic. From this, the cloudiness develops as an aftereffect. It is like when you get hit and then you get dizzy afterwards.

Question. When you speak of "things as they are," do you mean completely without projections? It is at least theoretically possible to experience things without projections, isn't it? The reason I ask is because if there is an overwhelming quality to experiencing things as they are, then that sense of overwhelmingness would be a projection, wouldn't it?

Rinpoche. It is definitely possible to experience things without projections. But just things as they are would not be overwhelming. That is dualistic. There would be no quality of overwhelming because overwhelming means "who has got control over who." So the question of overwhelmingness does not arise at all.

Seeing things as they are is very, very plain. Because it is so plain, it is colorful and precise. There is no game involved, therefore it is more precise, clearer. It does not need any relative supports; it does not call for any comparisons. That is why the individuality of things is then seen more precisely—because there is no need to compare anything to anything. You see the merit of each situation in its own right, as it is.

Question. Is not the student of abhidharma always playing a game then, intellectually assuming a nondualistic point of view and then using that to actually work through duality?

Rinpoche. That is not so much the case with the abhidharma. I would say that is more true of working with the sunyata principle according to the middle way or madhyamika school of Buddhism. This is a philosophy which developed after the abhidharma. Another example would be the koan practices in the Rinzai tradition of Zen where the meditation involves trying to use a certain kind of logic which is apparently illogical. But it *is* a logic of its kind because it is illogical. Using the koan again and again exhausts the mind's habitual thinking and takes one off the road somehow. There is a sudden experience of the futility and child-ishness of trying to apply ordinary logic, and that is where the gap or *satori* comes. In that case it is using a kind of logic of nonduality dualistically in order to destroy dualism.

On the other hand, the abhidharma merely presents some first idea of the pattern of duality. It is like a philosophy of meditation. By explaining the psychological pattern, it tells why meditation is valid.

Question. With regard to the eight consciousnesses—does it make sense to try to have a direct experience of any one of them isolated from the rest, or is this too abstract a way of going about it?

Rinpoche. I think that is too abstract. You cannot deal with them purely individually. It is like looking at a person: if you look at a person from the point of view of how fat or how thin he or she is, you still cannot fail to see also that person's head and toes and what clothes he or she is wearing. So in looking at experience from one perspective you see the rest as well. Once we experi-ence one sense consciousness, then what gives that particular sense consciousness the quality of consciousness relates it to the others. Each sense consciousness, to a certain extent, contains the overall picture. It must be what it is in relation to some back-ground; it must breathe some air to survive. It is like seeing a flower growing—when you see the flower, you also see the ground it is growing out of.

Question. Is everything we experience within the basic igno-rance, within the eighth consciousness, including wisdom or higher states of meditation?

Rinpoche. Yes. That is precisely why the whole thing is hopeful, precisely why it is worthwhile looking into our state of mind.

Question. So then higher states of meditation don't blank out the six senses, for example?

Rinpoche. Not at all. Of course not. In fact the six sense consciousnesses are heightened. If we regard meditation as just getting into a fog so that you do not see, you do not feel, some-thing is terribly wrong. In that case meditation would reduce one to a zombie. The enlightened man would have to be rescued. Someone would have to feed him and take him to the bathroom. We would have to have an enlightenment ward.

Question. Rinpoche, you spoke of ignorance as not being willing to go back. What is the way back; is it meditation?

Rinpoche. One is not willing to trace back how one came to be ignorant. But actually one cannot go back literally. One does not really have to go back. Rather one discovers what one was by the process of going more deeply into the present situation. That is the difference between an intuitive approach and an intellectual one. You can go back intellectually, but that does not help; you remain stuck in the same point of view. The whole idea is that if you are able to realize what you are at the present moment, you do not need to try to go back. What you are at this moment contains the whole message of what you were. That is really the practice of nonduality in meditation—seeing your present situation and going with it, identifying with the particular sense experiences of sight, smell and so on. Just experience the simplicity of them.

Question. I don't understand the first skandha. It seems it would be more basic than experience itself if it is more basic than the second and third skandhas of feeling and perception and the rest of them.

Rinpoche. The first skandha of form is basic, yes. Feeling and perception and the rest of the skandhas are built out of that basic thing. They are different types of attributes of form, so to speak, that are around it.

Question. Is there any activity within that world of form? It seems to me that the most basic activities I ever experience begin with feeling.

Rinpoche. No, what you are talking about is what you might call "facade experience." Fundamental experience begins with relativity, with the notion of comparison, which means ego and its projections. You cannot experience anything without a somebody to experience it and that is the starting point. That somebody is an unknown person, but experiencing it feels good. That is ignorance and the ego.

Question. So the first step is naming and labeling in order to begin experiencing yourself.

Rinpoche. Yes, yes—one's own position. The starting point of comparison.

Question. What is a skandha?

Rinpoche. Skandha means "heap." It is a collection, pile. That means it is not an independent definite object like a brick, but a collection of a lot of little details and aspects of psychological inclinations of different types. For instance, the second skandha, feeling, is not solid, not one feeling. It contains all sorts of feelings. The third skandha, perception, is the same—it is a collection. So ego is made out of a lot of particles rather than being one fixed thing that keeps going on.

Question. You say that the six sense consciousnesses are in the first skandha, the skandha of form. In the ordinary understanding, when one speaks of the senses one is already talking about perception; and yet perception is the third skandha.

Rinpoche. The senses are connected with perception; but there is more grasping and holding on involved in perception proper. Just the pure senses are very simple, mechanical almost.

Question. Could you give us a concrete example showing how the skandhas come into play—form, feeling, perception and so on? Something simple—for example, if I see a car.

Rinpoche. The process that takes place here takes place in a fraction of a second of consciousness, that lasts something like a five-hundredth of a second. First you have an impression of something. It is blank, nothing definite. Then you try to relate to it as *something* and all the names that you have been taught come back to you and you put a label on that thing. You brand it with that label and then you know your relationship to it. You like it or you dislike it, depending on your association of it with the past.

Now the very, very first blank, which may last a millionth of a second, is the meditation experience of the primordial ground. Then the next instant there is a question—you do not know who and what and where you are. The next moment is a faint idea of

18

finding some relationship. Then you immediately send your message back to memory, to the associations you have been taught. You find the particular category or the particular label you have been taught and you stamp it on. Then at once you have your strategy of how to relate with that in terms of liking it or disliking it. This whole process happens very quickly. It just flashes into place.

Question. Are all five skandhas in there?

Rinpoche. All five will be there, though I did not describe them all.

Question. Could you say more about the cloudy mind and the difference between the eighth consciousness, the seventh and the six sense consciousnesses?

Rinpoche. We begin with the eighth consciousness, the background, and then the seventh is kind of a way of relating the eighth consciousness to the six sense consciousnesses. But it is a very random way of relating because you no longer have any sense of direction, you do not know how to proceed. If sight comes first or sound or smell—it just happens to you. You are just insensate, just crawling along. The seventh consciousness is more intelligent than the eighth, than the basic ignorance, but you are still only sleepwalking, almost awake but not quite.

Question. Is that at all like when you find yourself walking in the garden and you hadn't realized you were there? You've done something without realizing it?

Rinpoche. Yes, it has actually been described that way. It is the subconscious feeling of a possible way of relating with the senses, but you have not quite worked it out properly yet. It happens in the midst of very precisely defined situations as well. It does not have to be a dreamy state at all. In those cases it is almost like the impact of the first bewilderment is coming to life again. But it still has a certain tinge of the dreamy quality and a potential of the six sense consciousnesses in it. It is a sort of no-man's land that you go through.

Question. Is this state characterized by a sense of tension between opposites, such as when for a minute you are confused between sweet and bitter? You are vacillating back and forth between the two and then you realize that the taste is just what it is?

Rinpoche. That sounds like when you have already gotten to the sense consciousnesses. But at the beginning you are not sure, you are just feeling around it. The seventh consciousness is like putting something in your mouth; chewing and tasting is on the level of the six senses.

FEELING

W E SHOULD PERHAPS GO ON TO THE NEXT STATE —the second skandha, feeling. Feeling consists of the pleasurable and the painful. In the usual psychology of people, pleasurable experiences are related to as positive and creative and painful experiences are related to as negative and destructive. This development of relating to things in terms of positive or negative value is an extension of the basic pattern of ego established by form, the first skandha. Having already the basic form, something definite and solid to hold onto, we go a little beyond that to trying to identify that form as friend or enemy, hostile or welcoming. This has the effect of solidifying whatever it is even further as something that defines ego's position by implication. Form provides a background which is composed of rudimentary names and concepts— positivity, good feeling, godliness, cleanliness, beauty, power and so on on the one hand; and the negative, painful, evil, dirty, destructive and so on on the other hand. The first is connected with birth, the second with death. These dualistic criteria, or others such as hot and cold, are the starting point for feeling. Feeling, in the sense of the second skandha, cannot function independently of them.

Feeling in this sense is something much more fundamental than just pure sensation. All kinds of concepts develop on the basis of feeling's basic dualism. Fundamentally it is of the nature of positive and negative, but feeling also has the third possibility of indifference.

The positivity and negativity of feeling is elaborated in terms of the mind/body situation. Feeling solidifies itself in terms of these two fields of experience. Feeling relates to mind as emotions and to body as clusters of instincts, things, thingness. Understanding of the mind/body pattern of feeling is very important in connection with meditation. We can meditate either intellectually or intuitively. Meditation on the intellectual level is involved with the mind side of mind/body; it is very imaginary. Intuitive meditation engages the body level of feeling, particular bodily sensations—pleasurable sensations, pain in the legs, hot and cold temperatures in the room and so on.

Mind is the emotional, imaginary or dream quality. And body, in this case, is also a quality of mind. That is, we do not, in feeling, experience body as it is. We experience *our version* of body. The fundamental point of view of ego based on comparative criteria, the definite separation between this and that, is already operational at this point. That basic twist is already there with the first skandha, form. The unobstructed space of things as they are is already distorted by the time we get to feeling. We cannot help anyway working along with this situation as naive people confronted by what has happened already. Still, looked at from a very basic point of view, the whole involvement of feeling is very childish. In fact, when we really see it, we see it is fundamentally deceptive.

When we talk about feeling, we usually think in terms of feeling towards someone else: you fall in love with someone, you are angry with someone. In that imagery the other person is all-important and you are insignificant. On the other hand: you feel slighted or you want to be loved. In that case you are all-important and the others are insignificant. Feeling plays that introvert-extrovert game of making itself important by reflecting off of "other." But in reality all that is very remote. Nobody is actually involved but yourself. You are alone and are creating the whole game by yourself.

So understanding feeling is very revealing about how you relate with things. Feeling involves the pretense that you are involved with somebody; but actually you are just beating your own head against a wall. You constantly search further and further thinking you are going to get at something, but ultimately, still, you are beating your head against a wall. There is no answer to feeling's search, no savior for it.

That is why the buddhadharma is an atheistic teaching. We have to accept that ours is a lonely journey. Studying the second skandha of feeling can be extremely important in helping us to realize that the whole journey is made alone, independent of anybody else. Still we are trying to beat ourselves against something all the time.

So to return to the mind/body development of feeling, the mind aspect of it provides tremendous resources for this delusive process, inexhaustible sources of dreaming and imagining. This extends to the situation of using drugs such as LSD and others which can produce all kinds of seemingly visionary and creative experiences. Experiences of perpetual unfolding of sight, smell, sound—beautiful like the continuous unfolding of a flower—can be produced. This kind of feeling on the mind level—in ordinary situations, in the drug experience, in meditation—provides all kinds of occasions for dwelling on spiritual materialism. Spiritual materialism means relating to experiences in terms of their possible benefit to ego, which is a quality of all the skandhas. Spiritual materialism tends to associate anything to do with spirituality with a dream world or heaven, with something that has nothing to do with the body situation, with something that altogether bypasses the kitchen sink.

The body aspect of feeling is associated with actual relationship with things. This element becomes much more vivid in the next skandha, perception, which we will discuss further on. This experience of actual things, thingness, of solidity and stability—as I have already said, this is not solidity and stability as it is, but our version of it. We *think* it is solid, we *think* it is thing. Still, relating with this body aspect of feeling is spiritually very provocative and open.

Feeling

Suppose suddenly we get sick and feel pain in our body. The body is a thing made out of all kinds of things; therefore pain in us makes us feel a relationship with actual reality rather than imagining anything beyond it. Of course in this kind of situation there is always the likelihood that somebody will come sit by our bed and read us prayers of how beautiful the beyond would be if we could only get out of this shameful, raw physical situation. Talking about the beauties of heaven and spirituality, the person hopes to get us drunk on it and get our mind off the bodily situation of pain. But that does not work. Once we are into the world of imagination in which we can imagine how beautiful beyond-the-body could be, we are also connecting up with the imagination of how terrible the pain could become. We are lost in the world of wishful thinking or unwanted thoughts. Somehow relating directly with the body aspect of feeling goes much more in the direction of what is.

Question. I really don't understand. In the beginning you said that feeling could only function independently if it had concepts to work with, to relate itself to. Then right after that, when you mentioned mind and body, I thought right away that these are the concepts it's relating itself to in order to be independent. Is that true?

Rinpoche. Well, the feeling happens with the concept, but as it happens that whole movement becomes bewildering and the concept does not apply any more. Actually pain and pleasure, apart from the second skandha, just happen. They have nothing to do with concepts or criteria at all. Pain or pleasure does not have to be a comparative thing. There could be independent pain, independent pleasure. We can afford to experience pain and pleasure without feeling. Many people might feel this is extremely demonic, that if there are no strings attached, if feeling does not have to be connected to concepts, you might be experiencing that through destroying or hurting people. But this fear on the part of

24

people of the demonic aspect of themselves comes from being afraid of an unknown situation. They are afraid of that space because they have not seen the other aspect of it that is without hope or fear. Once they get a glimpse of the possibility of pain and pleasure without hope and fear, they see it as demonic. Of course there is nothing to latch onto there. If you take away the hope and fear then pain and pleasure remains as it is. There is no way of relating with it except directly.

Question. So mind and body—one is not pain and the other pleasure, but both are sort of organs of pain and pleasure? Is that it?

Rinpoche. Well, yes. But at the same time mind is more closely connected with pleasure, because mind invites imagination. It invites imagination about what might be good, it is hopeful about possibilities of gaining something. But body is very much down-to-earth; it constantly brings us back to what we have to face. It's like the difference between taking the whole family to the theater or movies, which is the mind situation, and when we come back home and have to clean up our old dishes and cook a meal, which is the body situation.

Question. Rinpoche, I don't understand, because it seems that the imagination is just as inclined, in fact probably more inclined, toward the imagination of pain than the imagination of pleasure.

Rinpoche. Well, you see, the whole point is that imagining pain and pleasure as a solid thing is not very appealing. But on the other hand imagining pain and pleasure as a floating situation is much more appealing, because you can turn pain into pleasure in your imagination. You see the difference? In other words, nobody likes to face reality. The reality is physical, the body, the form of the first skandha that we created at the beginning. We have a body, "I am what I am." It's like an individual God-consciousness.

Once you have that thing, "I am what I am," then it becomes very solid.

Question. So physical pain, then, could be translated into pleasure if it is seen as strengthening the "I am"?

Rinpoche. All pain for that matter. You see, all sorts of doublecrosses can take place. You are sitting down to meditate and you say to yourself, "I'm going to do it for twenty hours starting right now; and whatever physical pain comes up is fine. It will be part of it. Okay, let it come through. Let it happen all along. That will be okay." And each time when pain comes you feel that you are overcoming the possessiveness of ego by feeling that particular pain. But in actual fact, by the time you finish your twenty hours of meditation, your ego has been strengthened because you feel that you worked so hard and you faced so much. You have been doublecrossed by ego.

Question. Is it possible to purify the feelings so that movement towards what is true feels good and movement towards what is not true does not feel good?

Rinpoche. The question is whether or not we see that there is no point in playing the game of feeling which is the second skandha. If we see that, we are not concerned by that or this any more. We go along very boldly, in a very stubborn way—we just sail along. We have our own plough, our own tank, and we are going to drive right along. Whether we are confronted by a house, a shop or a supermarket, we are going to drive right on through. The whole point seems to be whether or not we have that bold attitude of being what we are and are willing to disregard the duality of that and this. We accept our negative side and the fact we are a fool. Okay—that's fine. We use it as part of the meditational process.

26

Feeling

Nevertheless we are going to go on and on and on being ashamed or being proud of it. But we are just going to go on and on and on.

Question. Rinpoche, I wonder if I've misunderstood. Are there basically four kinds of feeling, bodily pleasurable and painful and mind pleasurable and painful?

Rinpoche. There seem to be, on one hand, pleasurable and painful feelings and, on the other hand, bodily and mental type feelings. The bodily feelings seem to be very complicated in a sense or very subtle, because it is very difficult to relate with a particular bodily pleasure or pain. This is because so much imagination is involved. To put it in terms of a very simple metaphor, the mind aspect of feeling is like being high on marijuana or LSD; and the body aspect is like being high on alcohol. The first is highly imaginary, the second is rather earthy but at the same time emotional. So it's like two kinds of intoxication—high on chemicals, high on yeast. Feeling has all kinds of variations—more than four. Pain, pleasure, or indifference could be friend or enemy, mental or physical.

You see, all human experience is high on something. Whether we regard ourselves as sober or not, we are constantly drunk, drunk on one thing or another, drunk on imagination or drunk on conflicts on the bodily level. Otherwise we could not survive. So we could say that this idea of feeling is different kinds of intoxication. You are intoxicated with good and bad: intoxicated with good, godliness, spirituality, pleasure; intoxicated with bad, evil, destruction, pain. You are intoxicated in imagination—all sorts of imaginations are going on. You are intoxicated in the body in that you are irritated by that and this and therefore you would like to get revenge by imposing yourself on something, laying your trip on something. The whole thing, all of experience, is being intoxicated on something. That is a very important and revealing aspect of this question of feeling, of this second stage in the development of the skandhas. The first skandha is ignorance, bewilderment, confusion and vague name and form. In the second one, already having some vague concept of where you stand, you would like to lay trips on something. This is what the feeling that happens—good and bad, body and mind—is about.

Question. Is every feeling dualistic?

Rinpoche. If it's based on something, some concept or wishful thinking. You see, every feeling of that sort must have a target in terms of this and that, of this in relation to that. This where I begin and that where I want to get to. As long as feelings are involved with this and that, that is duality. In other words, in relating to this and that, you have no way at all of relating with yourself. You have lost yourself altogether because you are so fascinated with this and that.

Question. You talked about the lonely journey and said that everything we do with other people is just projections, chasing our projections. So why do we need to relate with other people? It seems the obvious solution is just not to relate.

Rinpoche. "Why" and "why not" are saying the same thing. Do you see what I mean? "Why so" and "why not" are the same thing. So then, why don't we just plunge in?

Question. I seemed to understand that earthly intoxication is better than heavenly? Is bodily feeling, then, somehow more helpful?

Rinpoche. I think so, yes. Like the situation of a fistfight or making love—that kind of boiling situation brings you very much into the present moment.

Question. Rinpoche, you speak of a heavenly trip which tries to elude pain, move away from the down-to-earth situation and say that this is associated with pleasure. Is there a kind of intoxication which transcends the duality of pain and pleasure?

Rinpoche. I think so; but that is not associated with heaven; that transcends heaven in the sense of that which is above as opposed to you below experiencing it. As long as you relate to heaven above and you down below, you do not experience it properly, you do not transcend. But when you see that heaven is below, or that it is nowhere, that is the point where you transcend the whole process. That becomes an open and ultimate state, because then you are relating with the primordial ground. The primordial ground contains everything without being based on the relative situations of good and bad, this and that.

PERCEPTION

FEELING'S RELATING PROCESS consists of extremes, of polarities, dichotomies. In other words, one cannot develop feelings unless there are two extremes of some kind. Following from that, because of having some sense of taking sides with this extreme as opposed to that extreme, the subtleties of feeling have a solid, grasping quality in dealing with the projection of the world outside, rather than responding purely and directly. It is like a personal relationship with somebody which is based solely on temperamental reactions. As we know, there has to be something more than that, otherwise the relationship will not last very long. But feeling is like that. Feelings have a bouncy quality of jumping from one extreme to another. Having already the basic qualities of form, one starts to relate, to insert oneself into certain situations, into the two extremes of good and bad, pain and pleasure, body and mind, and so on. It is like in rock climbing when you insert a metal peg. That is the feeling. But to continue the climbing you have to have rope running through that peg. The rope that you have to have running through the pegs is perception, the third skandha. Perception is necessary so that the two extremes have something continuing underneath as a common link, a common thread that runs between happiness and sadness of body and mind.

Perception is based on that which is manifested by form and feeling and that which is not manifested by them. These are the two basic qualities in perception. In the first case, something is manifested via the six sense organs. You perceive something and you relate to it; you hold onto certain senses and their perceptions, and then from there you relate with that content. That is the first touching and feeling process. Feeling is like a radiation radiating out. Within that radiation, perception takes place as the radiation begins to function as definite details of that and this.

In this case "feeling" is not quite our ordinary notion of feeling. It is not the feeling we take so seriously as, for instance, when we say, "He hurt my feelings." This kind of feeling that we take so seriously belongs to the fourth and fifth skandhas of concept and consciousness. Here, in the case of the second skandha, it is the immediate, impulsive type of feeling of jumping to certain conclusions and trying to attach oneself to them. Perception could be called another type of feeling, the deepened feeling of experiencing that which is manifested and that which is not manifested in terms of the solid bodily situation.

You see, the whole idea of the manifested or the nonmanifested here comes from freezing space in our way of dealing with situations. Primordial consciousness flashes out, the unconscious flashes out, which creates tremendous open space. Within that space, ignorance and energy develop as we discussed before. Immediately, then, when ego begins to take up its position through the action of the skandhas, there is a natural automatic tendency to relate to that open space as overcrowded. Ego tries to possess that open space, that awakened state, by overcrowding it. But it can't overcrowd it with a lot of stuff, because there isn't enough stuff at that point; ego is not yet fully developed with all its resources of imagination. It is still the first impulsive situation of ego's development, so in order to crowd that space, one tries to freeze the whole space into a solid block. It's like water freezing into ice. The space itself is regarded as a solid thing of ego. In other words the principle of sunyata and nothingness, emptiness and openness, the awake state, is automatically in itself regarded as a sleep state, as overcrowded space. That kind of freezing of the space starts at the level of form, continues with feeling and now manifests fully with perception.

Perception, in the sense of the third skandha, cannot exist without solidness, without solidifying. That is the manifestation aspect. The nonmanifestation aspect is the aspect of annihilation, giving up all hope of retaining any kind of ground, which is based on fear. The first is hope, the second fear. The manifestation, physical manifestation, the solidified content of perception, is based on hope. And the second aspect, nonmanifestation, is based on despair (disappear). That works by, when there is no hope of maintaining solid ground anymore, making that position of despair into solid ground.

A third and fourth aspect of perception after manifestation and nonmanifestation are involved with criteria again. The criteria here concern how much area the grasping of perception can cover. Ego is extending its territory as far as it can, that is, trying to label and define as much as it can. Automatically the notions of big and small, greater and less, develop. Even the notion of smaller can help define more ground. So these polarities develop.

Then the fifth aspect of perception is absolute nothingness. Absolute nothingness in this case could be said to be a spark of intelligence coming through, connected with the primordial ground. There was a dispute on that subject between scholars of two schools of thought. One school said it was a spark of intelligence coming through. The other said that it was still confusion, that there could be no question of awakened intelligence in the skandhas; at this state of perception there could be no hope of freeing oneself at all. But, in my view and as I have been taught, there is a possibility of a complete change in one's perspective in relation to perception. An experience of absolute nothingness means giving up even hope itself or fear itself, and no longer perceiving in terms of grasping or clinging onto something. In that experience you are just trying to be brave enough to let go of your grasping a little to just feel around openly a bit in local areas, float around a little bit. So that aspect of perception means beginning to be pretty brave. This sort of bravery comes from *tathagatagarbha*, buddha nature, the basic intelligence. It is the

33

basic intelligence which begins to show this bravery. On the whole, any notion of exploring or taking a chance in relating with one's ego and projections is regarded as inspired by the enlightened mind. That is because you are not trying to hold on, to continue something, to prove something, but you are looking at other possibilities. That in itself is a very brave attitude and a very spacious one, because your mind is completely charged with curiosity and interest and space and questions. It is a sort of wandering process and is very hopeful and very positive in this particular connection. This absolute nothingness is the last stage of development of perception.

On the whole, the relationship between perception and the previous skandhas is that form creates the ego and ignorance and basic things, and feeling brings the spike quality or sharpness within that, of something trying to maintain itself. The perception comes as extending ego's territory and trying to define its position even much more. There is in perception a lot of referring back to the central headquarters of ego, and then extending and exploring further and further always in relation back to it. This establishment of territory in relation to a central reference point seems to be the general pattern of the development of ego.

Question. I only got four developments in perception. Manifestation, nonmanifestation.

Rinpoche. Big is the third one, and small is the fourth. The fifth is absolute nothingness.

Question. Could you go over nonmanifestation again?

Rinpoche. It has to do with fear. It is based on the fear of not having a solid situation anymore. Solidified space is hope. It is hopeful in that you manage to solidify the space as something to hang onto. In nonmanifestation, you have found nothing, and there is complete despair and giving up hope. But that is in itself a doublecross of ego, because giving up hope is in itself clinging to something.

Question. So in the case of manifestation I'm very taken up by the things I can see around me, whereas in nonmanifestation I'm more occupied by the things that I can't see that I wish were there.

Rinpoche. By the frustration of it. In nonmanifestation you are occupied with the frustration of not having what you want.

Question. And those two, hope and fear, would continually recreate each other?

Rinpoche. Yes, definitely, Wherever there is hope there is also survival of hope, which is based on fear. Maintenance of the hope is based on the fear of its nonfulfillment.

Question. What's the difference between big and small? Big and small what?

Rinpoche. The third and fourth ones are just two polarities. It is connected with outside and inside—expanding your vision outward and exploring, deepening your vision inward. Certain scholars in Tibet have spoken of perception as "hungry perception." It is dying to look for new material to eat up. It is constantly looking for possibilities for hanging onto something. The development of big and small particularly corresponds to this hungry notion of perception. Perception is much hungrier than feeling, because feeling is already partly secured. In the case of feeling, we have a form, a solid thing, and then we radiate out from the form, we extend and stretch ourselves, exploring very gently, very gently. But when we reach the level of perception, this sort of forced gentility begins to wear out and we become a bit desperate.

Question. Would these five parts of perception ever be simultaneous or are they separate psychological stages?

Rinpoche. It seems that they are separate psychological stages because you can concentrate on only one at a time. You see, the five skandhas are a very evolutionary thing. Form and feeling can manifest by themselves quite spontaneously, but when we get to perception and samskara, there are more and more separate things involved.

Question. I don't understand the evolutionary quality. I thought that all the skandhas had to work together, so that even though we speak of form first, it's not possible without perception, for example.

Rinpoche. That is true also, yes.

Question. You said form and feeling can exist on their own, but in order for there to be form, don't you have to perceive it?

Rinpoche. Yes, you definitely have to. What's wrong?

Question. Well, you say, "that comes later on" or "when we get to such and such skandha" as if that was the order of being, that we form and then we feel and then we perceive. But aren't they happening simultaneously?

Rinpoche. Well, it depends on our notion of time, of "simultaneously." We described the other day how the first stage of ego and its extensions develop by thousandths of a second. In that way the whole thing develops by stages. But on that time scale, you could also say they happen simultaneously. So that process happens simultaneously or progressively. There is a beginning and an end, but the application of notions of time becomes rugged and crude here. When we get to the level of consciousness, the last skandha, it becomes cruder still. That last skandha contains form and feeling and perception and samskara; but as far as the way of flashing is concerned, there is the evolutionary pattern. The first flash is the form and the next, feeling. As you flash further and further, the content becomes more and more involved. When you flash perception, that contains feeling and form; when you flash consciousness that contains all the other four.

Question. So the first flash of seeing something hasn't reached the stage of perception yet because it's without feeling?

Rinpoche. The first flash is just blank. Then a question, then an answer, then solidifying that and relating to it in terms of love and hate and so on. But very quickly, in a fraction of a second.

Question. Is it possible to continue to exist without this process? It seems if that would stop, I would be in great danger.

Rinpoche. That is what you think. There are people who have managed to do without it. After all, all this information about this pattern of the five skandhas comes from the point of view of those who have seen it from above, from an aerial view. It is not necessary to go through these complicated patterns of skandhas. It would be extremely simple not to go through them any more. You do not have to keep giving birth to the whole process. You can just perceive and go along with that perception, whatever arises.

Question. Is that kind of perception you were just talking about outside the ego's confine?

Rinpoche. Well, that becomes inspiration. Outside of ego, perception becomes inspiration. But that is getting onto the tantric level, which may be too difficult to understand.

Question. Inspiration for what?

Rinpoche. For that. Itself.

Question. It seems that there are hints of tantric teachings in all of this.

Rinpoche. Of course, yes; if it were without connection to the earlier teachings tantra would be a solitary planet. Actually some of the details of tantric iconography are developed from abhidharma. Different colors and feelings of this particular consciousness, that particular emotion, are manifested in a particular deity wearing such-and-such a costume, of certain particular colors, holding certain particular sceptres in his hand. Those details are very closely connected with the individualities of particular psychological processes.

Question. If you understand the abhidharma really clearly you can get into tantra, then?

Rinpoche. Yes, that is what happens. Actually a great deal of the tantric symbolism, the mandala, for example, is based on the terminology of the abhidharma. It runs right through. The abhidharma is a way of seeing; the psychology that it describes is not just a lump sum, a theoretical generality. There is individuality in every aspect of human emotion, human psychology. It is very rich. Each aspect of mind has its own individuality, and as you go along further and further, deeper and deeper, you begin to see these individual aspects as really living forces. At that point you also lose ego, because you no longer have to label experiencing as one big lump sum of "me" and "mine" and "I" anymore. That has become useless, absurd.

Question. Does one identify with these details? Is there a technique of identification happening?

Rinpoche. Well, if you identify with all these details going on in personal experience, that is very much a shortcut. You don't have to look for outside answers, because answers are there already. It happens on a personal level.

Question. What is the process when you say "identify with something"? Say I'm sawing a piece of wood, and I remember to identify with that, is it somehow like putting my mind on my hand? How does this fit in with the skandhas? Is it like connecting the sixth or the seventh or the eighth type of consciousness with the visual consciousness?

Rinpoche. You are quite right to raise that question. It is quite dangerous actually when we talk about identifying. You could identify outwardly with things as they are, so there is no center, but just fringe everywhere, expansion everywhere. Or you could identify inwardly, that is, you could identify with things that are happening with yourself as a solid entity.

Identification should be open identification, centerless identification, in other words, without a watcher. That is the whole point. If there is no watcher, then identification becomes real identification, really making a connection with things as they are. Whereas if you identify inwardly then you are identifying in accordance with some concept, in accordance with your own categories.

Question. Identifying inwardly would be connecting your mind with the thing?

Rinpoche. With the thing, a solidified notion, yes. That is what we call materialism, spiritual or psychological materialism.

Question. What is the other kind? Identifying outwardly is just being aware of what's happening, without any—

Rinpoche. Well, you are not watching your body and your physical motion of sawing wood, but you just become one with wood itself. You do not watch yourself being identified, but you become completely one with the action or object of what you are doing.

Question. What about when Buddha taught the woman at the well how to feel the rope and attend to the motion of drawing water? What about the practice of mindfulness?

Rinpoche. That is like using the breathing in meditation, it is the motion of the two arms—as outsiders. It has nothing to do with me and my arms, but it is just two arms doing a regular functional thing—drawing up water.

Question. So there is nothing built up that way? No territory or sense of ownership?

Rinpoche. Nothing is built up that way. Breathing is just breathing happening there. It has nothing to do with *my* breathing, so that I should have to breathe specially.

Question. Becoming one with the wood, is that becoming intoxicated?

Rinpoche. We could say that, yes. Once you are in the experience there is some logical pattern to follow, which becomes a sort of perpetually creative process; you begin to see the colorfulness, the vividness of things.

Question. Could you explain the relationship between fear and identification?

Rinpoche. Well, identification is surrendering and not referring back; not checking back with central headquarters but just going on with what is there. Fear is referring back to yourself and making sure that your relationship with what is happening is quite secure. If you don't check up on yourself, you might have to panic. Suddenly you stop identifying because you fear something is wrong—you begin to lose your grip. This is because in identifying, the carpet of security is pulled out from under your feet.

Question. Rinpoche, you said that nonmanifestation is based on fear, whereas it seems to me that the quality of fear is a more solid thing than hope. I see something more spacious about hope than fear. I don't understand how nonmanifestation is based on fear.

Rinpoche. Well, nonmanifestation is based on fear in the sense that it becomes despair. Fear projects a situation in which there is nothing to hang onto and you have lost every contact, every connection; so you are dwelling on that—which is despair. It is creating another type of ground to hand onto, dwelling on fear, enjoying fear or sadness as an occupation.

Question. Why is there a problem about this fifth state of perception, absolute nothingness, that some schools of Buddhism would consider this to be a cloudy mind or a clinging mind?

Rinpoche. I think there was tremendous distrust in the definition of the absolute, of absolute mind, buddha nature, and its intelligence. That connects with our previous discussion about viewing Buddha as a great scholar. From the point of view where being enlightened is being a great scholar, any kind of feeble intelligence or feeble inspiration is regarded as a manifestation of samsara. The people holding this view thought that in order to have a really good glimpse of the absolute you had to have fantastic dramatic flashes. They themselves had not had these experiences, but they imagined that should be the case. The other school, our school, says that awakened mind has to be something that is part of our everyday domestic experience of ego. The experience of awakened mind is extremely simple; it does not have to be dramatic. The faintest expression of intelligence is part of the awakened state of mind. So you do not have to build up a mythical notion of enlightened experience. It is something realistic and flashes of it happen constantly. That viewpoint also coincides with the tantric teachings.

Question. So all through these skandhas, the awakened state of mind is the thread that everything goes on, and somehow the complications built up by each skandha live on this thread which they obscure.

Rinpoche. That's right, that happens all the way along.

Question. So that the awakened state of mind is actually doing all the work that everything else is living on?

Rinpoche. Exactly, I mean even uprisings, agitation, aspects of living in the samsaric world like guerilla warfare and political intrigues and everything—all are based on a fundamental sense that something is not right, and seeing that something is not right is based on intelligence.

Question. So doubt is intelligence.

Rinpoche. Doubt is intelligence, yes. That is really very powerful thinking actually. The chaos is intelligence and it is teaching. So you do not have to ward off anything at all.

Question. Could you say something about pure pleasure and pure pain isolated unto themselves? How could they exist outside the body or mind?

Rinpoche. They cannot exist outside the actual body and the actual mind, but they can exist outside our version of the body and our version of the mind. That is the most difficult thing of all—we say "body" and we say "mind," but we have our own interpretation of them, our own concept of them, which constantly separates us from the reality of the body and mind, the bodyness, mindness, the thingness of things as they are. This thingness of things as they are is what is called "emptiness," sunyata, the actual isness quality of things. Things could be without us; they could remain pure and perfect as they are. But we put our own version over them, and we then amalgamate them all together. It is like dressing up dolls. We have the naked bodies and then we put on military costumes or monks' robes or an ordinary tie and suit. We dress them up. Then suddenly we find that they are alive. And we try to run away from them because they begin to chase us. We end up being haunted by our own desire and perceptions, because we put so much onto them. Finally our own creation becomes destructive to us.

Question. I really didn't understand what you said about freezing space.

Rinpoche. The basic ground is open ground, but you do not want to accept that. You want to solidify it to make it tangible, safe ground to walk on. So by freezing space, I mean solidifying that open space. There could be the experience of pain and pleasure as naked pain and naked pleasure without any problem of fixing them in relation to anything. We do not have to conquer our projections and our mind at all. We do not have to control anything. Things as they are can remain independent. Once situations are left open and fresh and naked, experience can become very flowing, real, living.

Question. Where do pure pain and pleasure come from in this pure, open situation?

Rinpoche. Well, they manifest by themselves. They are not

dependent on anything. That is the whole point. We do not have to have a chain-reaction process. Each pain and pleasure can come as an independent package deal. The whole problem arises from relating with experience as something other than just what it is. Then it has to be maintained or controlled. If you have extreme spiritual pleasure, there is the possibility of losing it or its dying because you are trying to maintain it. But really you do not have to maintain it, it is an independent, self-sufficient experience. Therefore, in the tantric iconography, pain and pleasure and all these experiences have been described as divinities, independent persons dancing on lotus seats. They are independent beings. They are not being manipulated by remote control.

Question. When you talk about pain and pleasure in their pure state, I think that if I tried to relate to that I would end up on a trippy imagination jag, leaving out the earth of the situation. I would just go off on a mind trip.

Rinpoche. I think that you might well as long as you have the aim and object of trying to get pure pain and pleasure. When you have that idea in mind and try to go out and do it, then you have to do something extraordinary, either take an acid trip or freak out. And you never make it because you have the idea in mind already prepared. That means that ego planned it for you and sent you out with its consent.

Question. Suppose you had a little flash of intelligence and then saw the whole process of ego starting all over again, the ego panicking and falling into a hungry-ghost mentality, cutting yourself off from the very thing that you want. What do you do with that process?

Rinpoche. If you see it happening, that is the key point, and you find some spontaneous way of dealing with it. It is like learning to swim. If you are suddenly pushed into the water, you automatically swim; whereas, after a certain time being educated in how to swim by teachers, watching becomes more of a hindrance than a help. Once you see the key point of the situation, then you can relate to it properly, actually do it.

You see the teachings are not really like "do-it-yourself" books. They do not go through every point down to the last detail. They just indicate, give hints. The teachings are an awakening process to rouse you to the situation, rather than a compendium of step-by-step, specific guidance. The teaching gives hints, and you are inspired to go out and develop them. Then you find that you can do it. That is the whole process. Spontaneity and basic intelligence become extremely important. They begin to function independently when the confusions begin to arise. That is what is meant by the notion of the universal guru.

INTELLECT

L OOKING AT THE GENERAL PICTURE of psychology as we
get involved with more and more complex patterns of the
skandhas, it becomes clear that it is a pattern of duality developing stronger and stronger. The general tendency of ego is
uncertain at the beginning how to establish its link with the
world, its identity, its individuality. As it gradually develops
more certainty, it finds new ways of evolving; it becomes more
and more brave and daring in stepping out and exploring new
areas of possible territory or new ways of interpreting and
appropriating the world available around it. So it is a pattern of a
kind of stubborn bravery making itself more complicated patterns. The forth skandha, *samskara*, is a continuation of this
pattern. It could be called "intellect." *Samskara* is intellect in the
sense of being intelligence which enables the ego to gather further territory, further substance, more things.

Samskara does not seem to have any good exact literal translation or equivalent term. The basic literal meaning has the sense of
a gathering or accumulation, meaning specifically a tendency to
accumulate a collection of mental states as territory. These mental states are also physical; they are mind/body states. So *samskara*
has quite a lot of varieties of different types of classifications of
mental patterns. But this is not just a series of names in a list; the
patterns are related to each other in an evolutionary pattern they
form together as well. The various aspects of *samskara* are mind/
body patterns that have different emotional qualities to them.
There are fifty-one general types of these. I do not think we have

to go to great lengths here to cover all the types in detail, but let me try to give you some rough idea of them.

There are certain samskaric patterns or attitudes associated with virtue or religion or goodness, which we could say are the expression of basic intelligence, buddha nature; but they also are appropriated by ego and so help constitute its natural tendency of spiritual materialism. There are eleven of these types of good attitudes or tendencies among which are surrendering or faith, awareness, discipline, equanimity, absence of passion, absence of anger, absence of ignorance, humbleness or shyness, a tendency of nonviolence, a tendency of energy or effort or bravery. An important point here is that nobody had to invent these religious or spiritual ideas, but they are a natural part of human psychology. There is a natural sort of gentleness, absence of aggression and passion, a hardworkingness and a nonviolence; and these tendencies develop as part of *samskara.*

Altogether the general nature of this particular group of samskaric tendencies is absence of aggression. They are a sort of dharma mind. By dharma we generally mean passionlessness in the sense of nongrasping or nonclinging. That which has a context of passion is nondharma. So these tendencies are characterized by an absence of speed or aggression. These thoughts are generally considerate thoughts. They contain a certain amount of conscience. They do not just exist arbitrarily, but they have some reason to be. For one thing there is the absence of aggression, openness, and for another thing this kind of mind/body pattern carries a high degree of awareness of the situations outside oneself. In other words, there is an absence of ego in the superficial sense; in the ordinary sense they are not egocentric. But this is not a question of the fundamental ego; such thoughts are not necessarily egoless. This depends on the user of the thoughts. However, the general quality of them reminds one of a good person, considerate and not egocentric in the ordinary popular sense.

Then there are the six opposite types of thoughts, the egocentric thoughts. They are ignorance, passion, anger, pride, doubt and dogmatism. These are considered to be the absence of the virtues of the kinds of thoughts we have just discussed.

Here again, the ignorance in question is quite different from the basic ignorance that constitutes the ego, that sort of fundamental ignoring oneself. The ignorance we are referring to here is the source of all the other kinds of evil thoughts, those which are not considerate, those which are the absence of the spiritual type of thoughts. They are characterized by a sort of sudden boldness which acts without considering the situation. They just act out on impulse, without any sharpness and precision. They are wholly intoxicated by a sense of whatever one wants to accomplish, so they act brashly without seeing one's relationship to the situation.

And passion here is also actual passion rather than the fundamental passion of grasping. It is the actualized passion of desire. Whereas the fundamental passion is sort of an innate quality of grasping within ego, this is the actual active movement of grasping. On this level, passion, hatred and pride are all directly active qualities rather than fundamental ones. Pride here is the sense of preservation of oneself in relationship with others. Doubt is the sense of not having enough security in oneself. Dogmatic belief is clinging onto a particular discovery that we have made and not wanting to let go of that idea because we feel if we did there would be nothing left to cling onto.

Dogmatic belief itself is divided into different types, for instance, the philosophical beliefs in eternalism and nihilism. Eternalism is the idea that everything, in the worldly or spiritual spheres, is continuous and permanent. Part of this is the notion that there is a permanent significance to our experience, that there could be an ultimate and permanent salvation within the realm of the experiencer. Nihilism is the opposite extreme. It is the fatalistic belief that everything has no value and is meaningless. Another of the dogmatic tendencies is the false belief in morality or a particular discipline that one follows, dogmatically clinging onto it and trying to hold onto it as a philosophical view.

Then there are four types of neutral thoughts; sleep or slothfulness, intellectual speculation, remorse and knowing. These are neutral in that they can fit in with different patterns, the virtuous or the evil ones. Theoretical intellectual speculation is obviously neutral in that it functions in the service of either kind of tendency. Remorse is in a sense a questioning process that further clarifies a situation: you have done something wrong and feel doubtful about it, which leads you on a kind of a process of rediscovery. That is neutral in that that process of discovery could function in relation to either the considerate or egocentric patterns. Knowing is a neutral state because when you learn something you have a sudden open attitude to it at that moment, before you get into the next double take, that is, before ego appropriates it as territory. There is that momentary open feeling of acceptance of whatever you heard, whatever you understood. Sleep or slothfulness is of course also neutral, since it also contains that kind of possibility of belonging to an open or egocentric context.

Now all these kinds of thoughts are further classified according to the instinctive behavior connected with them, how you project them to the world outside. That is done on the basis either of hatred or desire. Hatred in this case is a natural kind of aggression, and desire is a natural kind of longing. All these thoughts are motivated either by instinctive hatred or desire. Even apparently good thoughts, compassion, for instance, on the level of ego, would have an underlying sense of hatred or of passion. It depends on whether the thought process is originally based on speed or on a kind of starvation, which is the need to grasp something, to absorb oneself in something. In addition, some thought patterns have ignorance as underlying motivation.

The study of the samskara skandha can teach us that all the phenomena of human psychology, whatever types of thought patterns occur, all have these good and bad and indifferent qualities. Therefore we cannot really define one thought pattern as being the only right kind—there is no such thing as absolute aggression or absolute passion or absolute ignorance. All of them have the slight tendency of the other types. The whole idea is that therefore one cannot just condemn one type and totally accept another, even if it is the spiritual virtuous type of thoughts. They are questionable as all the other kinds of thoughts are questionable. That is a very important point—nothing is really to be condemned or accepted.

On a larger scale, the whole pattern of the five skandhas is also neutral, rather than belonging particularly to samsara or particularly to nirvana. But one thing is quite certain and constant about the five skandhas—they manufacture karmic chain reactions all the time. That is always, unquestionably the case. The karmic pattern cannot exist by itself, of course, since karma is not some other kind of entity that exists independently. Karma is a creative process which brings results, which in turn sow seeds of further results. It is like an echo process. You shout and your voice bounces back on you as well as being transmitted to the next wall, and it goes on and on. And the skandhas could be said to be the horse of karma. The speed of karma is based on the five skandhas. The natural, sort of chemical cause-and-effect pattern remains within karma, but the speed that the cause-and-effect process requires in order to function is the skandhas.

Perhaps we should have some discussion.

Question. Did you say that samskara is associated with neither nirvana nor samsara, or does that apply to all the skandhas?

Rinpoche. To all the skandhas.

Question. I am puzzled. You said that the good thoughts were somehow related to buddha nature.

Rinpoche. Well, that is easily possible if there is underlying nonego intonation. That is why they are called "good," because they are not acts of egomania in the literal, ordinary sense.

Question. Is there more possibility of buddha nature in the states of mind classified as good?

Rinpoche. Yes, there is a tendency to be closer to the awakened state; but at the same time if this good is being used by the ego, then it is not necessarily absolute good, but just sort of pseudo.

Question. Then does it make any difference? That is, is it worthwhile trying to be a good boy?

Rinpoche. I don't think so, necessarily. Although these are said to be the good or virtuous ones, at the same time such thoughts—patience or nonviolence or whatever—cannot happen by themselves. They have to have the tinges of passion or aggression, as I said, or also ignorance. They cannot constitute the basic energy that has to go along with them for them to occur. So there is no such thing as one hundred percent good in any case. The tendencies are sort of lighter and heavier rather than good and bad.

Question. So they all come from ignorance, hatred and passion.

Rinpoche. They do, yes.

Question. Is the thread that connects them perception, feeling or both?

Rinpoche. Quite likely it is form, the basic continuity, ignorance which makes it all possible for the others to continue.

Question. I am confused about speed. There is a speed of the ego being driven, going faster and faster, and there is also a speed of universal energy, or something like that. There is an evil speed but is there also another speed?

Rinpoche. Well, I'm trying to use the word speed as a sort of driving aggression. But that is not purely pejorative. This has a positive aspect as well, because any kind of aggression, any kind of movement that there is, always has neutral energy that goes along with it. So speed is pure force, neutral force, which could be used for different purposes. The buddha-wisdom of the accomplishment of all actions could also be called speed. But somehow that speed is not based on a target. Once you have a target, or criteria in terms of reaching somewhere from somewhere else, that makes the whole pattern of speed destructive. In the case of the energy without a target, without a relativity notion, that speed just happens and returns just by its own nature. It fulfills actions completely and comes back. Because fulfilling action in this case follows no criterion or model at all. The speed or energy just goes out and gets into the natural situation spontaneously, tries to bring the natural situation to its fullest state and then comes back. This kind of speed does not behave in a dictatorial way. In the case of ego speed, you have a blueprint of what should be happening and you put out speed accordingly. You try to control situations or remold them. That leads to disappointment and confusion.

Question. Wouldn't these dogmatic beliefs that you talked about be beliefs on the part of the "watcher"?

Rinpoche. If there is any tendency to get yourself to believe in certain ideas, particularly philosophical views such as the nihilistic and eternalistic ones, automatically you are aware of the learning process as being separate. You watch yourself in the process of learning and you use particular tools of different intensity, either gentle or aggressive ones, to bring about a certain result. So all these beliefs are in a sense very deliberate. It is a natural mind process, but that mind process involves deliberate effort—deliberately trying to be good or deliberately trying to grasp something and so on. Except for those four types of neutral patterns, sleep and the others: they are not deliberate, which is why they are called neutral. They can be influenced by either kind of deliberate thought patterns. They do not contain a watcher, actually. That is why they can be used by either kind of deliberate pattern or by ego or nonego. But the rest of them are fixed and definite.

Question. That watcher is the one that puts everything that happens into one of those categories, these samskaric types of good and bad?

Rinpoche. Yes. That is actually a certain kind of common sense developed by the establishment of ego. By this time ego is so well established, it has developed its own regulations and rules. This becomes a kind of common sense. You see, as long as you are involved with the ego game, all these flashes of different types of thoughts and concepts are not independent ones at all. They are purely dependent on central headquarters. You always have to report back to yourself in order to define the ground. That is the watcher. And the watcher has a watcher as well.

Question. Would you say a little more about doubt? You have just spoken of doubt as one of the negative factors. Previously you spoke about it in a positive sense.

Rinpoche. We have been speaking about two quite different kinds of doubt. One kind is one of the six types of egocentric thoughts. This is ego's tendency to have doubt in terms of the motivation of passion and anger and ignorance. It is a fear of losing ground, bewilderment rather than doubt in the intelligent sense. We fear we may not be able to survive to implement our ambition properly in the perspective of our egohood. It is more a fear of losing ground than doubt.

The intelligent doubt we were talking of earlier on is a general sense that there is something wrong all the way through; a sort of seed of doubt which runs right through the whole five-skandha process. It is the quality of inquisitiveness, questioning mind, which is the seed of the awakened state of mind. This is doubt or intelligence which is not protecting anything. It is purely questioning rather than trying to serve either the ego or nonego state. It is purely a process of critical view which goes on all the time.

Question. I'm trying to relate this to inner experience. Associations present themselves and many other things, you know, when one is sitting quietly. And then a thought happens and there is belief in it, and then remembrances, and then an impulse arises that this that I am believing is not necessarily so. It may or may not be. I think what I'm trying to ask is—is this still within the pattern of attachment, or is this in the direction of something a little bit more free?

Rinpoche. You see, it is very difficult to make a generalization. What you described in itself could have different implications. The implication could be based solely on a survival notion; it could be based on a sense of "maybe that one, maybe this one"— ego jockeying for better position. Or there is the possibility of something else—that it could be based on a kind of open mind. It depends on your own relation to that.

Question. You mentioned slothfulness as one of the neutral states. But I'm wondering in what way slothfulness can be converted. Can it be channeled in the same way that intellectual speculation could be clarified?

Rinpoche. Slothfulness could be sort of infiltrated rather than changed or channeled into something else. This is because slothfulness does not contain any definite thing. It is a process, a mind process of not having made up your mind quite. You are just trundling along. So it has the possibility of being infiltrated from any side.

Question. Is slothfulness synonymous with laziness?

Rinpoche. Well, the words are complicated in this case. Somehow, laziness could have the connotation of being a naughty boy. You know, you should be doing thus and such, but you do not want to do it. Sort of stubbornness. But sloth is a general heaviness or being sleepy rather than game playing. It is just quite honest and ordinary.

Question. So in that sense slothfulness may be more receptive, more passive?

Rinpoche. Precisely, yes. It could be infiltrated.

Question. Insofar as you try to be something, wouldn't it be better to try to be honest instead of trying to be good? I mean honest in the sense of trying to abandon one's own pretensions. Isn't that the basic effort?

Rinpoche. I think so, yes. The reason why all these different types of thoughts and ideas are being introduced, in fact, is so you can see your psychological picture in its fullest perspective; so that you do not try to regard one kind of thought pattern as good or another as bad; so that instead you regard everything directly and simply.

Question. I have an image going in my mind that the skandhas represent energy which has gone astray from the awakened state of mind and has taken on various forms. Lost from its origin, it

has taken on various forms. And it seems that spiritual understanding would return this lost energy to its origin in some way.
But also I have another image from when you pointed out that
ignorance or form was the thread that holds all the skandhas
together. Then I had the thought that it is simply a question of not
operating ignorance—if you're just completely still and uncon-
cerned it will all just blow away. And the two images give me two
different attitudes. Do you know what I mean?

Rinpoche. Well, I don't see any difficulties there. Ignorance is
the binding factor for all the skandhas in their minute detail,
but ignorance cannot exist by itself without relative situations,
and the relative situation of ignorance is the awakened state of
mind, intelligence, which makes ignorance survive or die. In
other words, we could say that the awakened state of mind is the
thread also, in the same way as ignorance. It runs right through
the skandhas.

Question. But it wouldn't be awakened if it was doing that.

Rinpoche. It would. Ignorance feels the other, the awakened,
aspect of the polarity; therefore it does what it does. There is
some subtle relationship ignorance is making with the basic intelligence of buddha nature. So ignorance in this case is not stupid, it
is intelligent. The term for ignorance in Tibetan, *marigpa*, means
"not seeing, not perceiving." That means deciding to not perceive, deciding to not see, deciding to not look. Ignorance makes
certain decisions and, having already made a certain decision, it
tries to maintain it no matter what. Often it faces a hard time
keeping to that decision constantly, because one act of ignorance
cannot persist indefinitely, once and for all. Ignorance also is
based on sparks or flashes of ignorance operating on some
ground, and the space between two sparks of ignoring is the intelligence that this process of ignorance is operating on. It also
happens occasionally that ignorance forgets to maintain its own

quality, so that the awakened state comes through. So a meditative state of mind occurs spontaneously when, occasionally, the efficiency of ego's administration breaks down.

Question. Would you explain what you mean by "ego game"?

Rinpoche. I think that is what we have been discussing all along in this seminar. The basic notion of ego is the notion of survival, trying to maintain oneself as "I am," as an individual. Now, as we just said, there is a tendency for the coherency of that occasionally to break down. Therefore one needs to find all sorts of means of confirmation, of confirming a coherent, consistent me, a solid me. Sometimes, quite knowingly, ego has to play a game as though nothing had gone wrong with it. It pretends seeing through ego never happened, even though secretly it knows better. So ego trying to maintain itself leaves one in the strange position of trying to indoctrinate oneself oneself. This is a false pursuit, of course. But even knowing it is false does not particularly help, because ego says, "That's not the point. We have to go on trying to learn to survive, playing this survival game of grasping, using any situation available in the present moment as part of the survival technique." This involves a power game as well, because at a certain stage the defense mechanisms you have set up become more powerful than you are. They become overwhelming. Then, when you become used to the overwhelming quality of the defense mechanisms, when, for a moment, they are absent, you feel very insecure. That game of polarities goes on and on. On the whole, ego's game is played in terms of ignoring what is really happening in a situation. You constantly, quite stubbornly want to see it from your point of view rather than seeing what really is happening there.

Question. You spoke of an aerial view of the five skandhas. Do you mean that with the development of meditative awareness one can actually experience the development of the skandhas in oneself?

Rinpoche. Yes. In a sudden glimpse of awareness, or in the meditation state, one sees the ups and downs of the five skandhas taking place and dissolving and beginning to develop again. The whole idea of meditation is to develop what is called the "wisdom eye," *prajñaparamita,* transcendental knowledge. It is knowledge, information, at the beginning, when you are watching yourself and beginning to discover yourself, your psychological pattern. And suddenly, strangely, that watching process begins to become an experiencing process, and it is, in a sense, already under control. That does not mean to say that the development of the five skandhas would stop taking place. The skandhas happen continuously until they are transmuted into what are called the "five tathagathas," the five types of awakened being.

You see, at the beginning, we have to develop a very sharp, precise mind to see what we are. There is no other way of sharpening our intelligence. Pure intellectual speculation would not sharpen it at all, because there you have to introduce so much stuff that blunts, that overclouds. The only way to do it is just to leave intelligence as it is with the help of some technique. Then the intelligence begins to learn how to relax and wait and allow what takes place to reflect in it. The learning process becomes a reflection rather than creating things. So waiting and letting what arises reflect on the intelligence is the meditation practice. It is like letting a pond settle down so the true reflection can be seen. There are already so many mental activities going on constantly. Adding further mental activities does not sharpen the intelligence. The only way is just to let it develop, grow.

Question. One of the six virtues of a bodhisattva is energy, exertion, *virya.* It is hard to relate this virtue to the idea of a waiting intelligence.

Rinpoche. Well, I don't see any problem, particularly. You see, hardworkingness or exertion does not necessarily mean doing a lot of things. Waiting in itself could be very hard work, being is very hard work, and there are so many temptations not to do it.

Question. Is there some kind of recognizable psychological event which particularly reinstigates the process of the five skandhas and of karma?

Rinpoche. Yes, that is what is called "immediate cause." It is the immediate occasion of getting into a further series of events, a sort of steppingstone. Each transition has to have that intermediary moment. Even in sleep things function that way. It allows you to fall asleep from being awake and in dreams pushes you from one moment to the next and then makes it possible to wake up again. Karma is dependent on that state, that immediate cause. It cannot function without it. The whole idea of the practice of meditation is that in the meditative state you do not have that impulse. That suddenness or the restlessness is automatically freed; that sudden impulse has been transmuted into a flowing process through the use of a meditation technique. That is how the process of meditation can be a way of preventing planting the seed of karma.

Question. It seems from what you've been saying that meditation in action has something to do with going very much into detail. You know something and then something else comes along. And if you could just go along with the new detail—

Rinpoche. Well, you see, awareness meditation, meditation in action, is a process of providing fundamental space. If you are talking or you are doing things, you are acting within that open space, so that no sudden jolt can happen, no sudden confusion or slothfulness. That abrupt clicking-in of confusion can only take place if the ground, the basic space, has been solidified or frozen.

The karmic process operates against that kind of solidified background. Whereas once that solidity has been transformed by acknowledging there is another aspect to it, which is open space, openness, then any kind of sudden, impulsive movement is accommodated. Still the same rhythm goes on, but that rhythm now becomes a creative movement. The rhythm of events goes on, but you appreciate that that rhythm can happen on space, on open ground, and this brings back the message of meditation happening.

So you do not have to force yourself to remember; you do not have to try to maintain your awareness all the time. Once you are open to the challenges of the moment, somehow, as you go along, the situation flashes back the awareness to you. So a perpetually creative process develops and a highly precise one as well.

Question. If the situation doesn't flash back that awareness, then you forget it?

Rinpoche. Well, you disown whatever comes up. If you try to keep up and maintain something, then it does not work. It becomes your product. You are solidifying space again.

Question. Getting back to that transitional moment in karma where it picks up impetus. Do I understand that as you advance in your meditation you notice this happening, and by noticing it you can prevent it from happening and control the situation? Once you notice what leads to the karma, do the steps become much easier to deal with?

Rinpoche. Well, that is rather tricky. Theoretically you might know the whole thing, but once you have the idea in mind that what you are doing is trying to escape from karma, to step out of it, then you are already doublecrossed. The probability then is that you are automatically not in the right state of mind. That is why is it important in meditation practice that at the time of practice everything is just based on a simple technique, but with no aim or object at all, none whatsoever. You give up everything and go along with the practice entirely and fully.

Question. Yes, but in daily situations I think it's helpful to deliberately notice things happening.

Rinpoche. You see, in daily situations if you have a certain understanding of the continuous quality of the meditation experience happening all the time, then, without trying to meditate deliberately, you automatically know the daily situation, because the daily situation comes to you as a reminder, rather than your trying to go to it. It becomes a perpetual creative process.

Question. You have talked about creation at times as though it were an ego process and now as though it is more egoless. Could you clarify?

Rinpoche. I suppose you could say there is ego creation and true creation. I think here again it is a question of whether or not the notion of competitive achievement, of an ideal or a goal is present. With ego's notion of creation you have a concept that you want to achieve something, and you try to match your situation with your idea of the actual achievement. You compare the dream and the actual reality. That is not the ultimate creative process but a one-way creation which can wear out. You build a thing and it is finished; you have no further place to go. It is a very limited inspiration.

Whereas in the other approach without aim and object, without a goal in mind, each situation acts as an end in itself. You go along with that situation and that situation brings another, it opens another possibility. So you go along and along. That is like the experience of the bodhisattva developing through the *bhumis* or stages of development. When one *bhumi* is accomplished, he goes on to the next. Without ambition he goes on and on. He has no desire for enlightenment, but one situation leads to another until he finds himself enlightened one day. This is because he relates to things on their own merits rather than in terms of a goal of his own.

So the ambition type of a creation is that of ego. The alternative is to have natural appreciation of creation itself rather than being fascinated by what *you* are doing. If you tune into the actual creativity itself, the delight of it, it becomes an inexhaustible source of creativity.

MEDITATION

PERHAPS AT THIS POINT there is a sense of being bombarded with the classifications of the abhidharma—the process of the development of the skandhas and the various aspects of form, feeling, perception and samskara. At this point I think it would be good to talk about the practice of meditation very practically and how it fits in with the psychological development we have been talking about. Meditation is a way of scientifically looking at our basic situation and seeing what is important in dealing with it. But maybe we think we do not have to deal with anything at all. Maybe we should just let everything happen and abandon the idea of meditating. That is another possibility, of course, a very tempting one. But the reason for getting into meditation is a very tempting one as well. If we get into meditation we begin to see our psychological situation very precisely and directly.

I think a fundamental problem that we all have is that we are very critical of ourselves to the point where we are even our own enemies. Meditation is a way of making up that quarrel, of accepting ourselves, making friends with ourselves. We may find we are not as bad as we have been told we are. We will also find that meditation practice is not something exotic and high out of reach so that we cannot grasp it. Meditation practice is something that takes place on a personal level. It involves an intimate relationship with ourselves. Great intimacy is involved. It has nothing to do with achieving perfection, achieving some absolute state or other. It is purely getting into what we are, really examining our actual psychological process without being ashamed of it. It is getting into what we are properly and thoroughly. It is just friendship with ourselves.

Unless we are able to make friends with ourselves there is no hope at all. If we abandon ourselves as hopeless, as villains, then there is no steppingstone. If we take that attitude then we must constantly be looking for something much better than ourselves. And that attempt to outrace ourselves on the spot can continue perpetually, on and on and on. And in fact that is just what we do.

So meditation is coming into contact with the actual situation of ourselves, the raw and rugged, painful, irritating, disgusting things going on within our state of being. But even if our state of being is disgusting we should look into it. It is beautiful to see it. To discover that such things exist in the natural situation is very beautiful. It is another dimension of natural beauty. People talk about appreciating natural beauty—climbing mountains, seeing giraffes and tigers in Africa and all sorts of things; but nobody seems to appreciate this kind of natural beauty of ourselves. This is actually far more beautiful than flora and fauna, far more fantastic, far more painful and colorful and delightful and all the rest.

Meditation is getting into this kind of natural situation, the organic natural situation of what we are, directly, thoroughly, properly. In order to do this, we cannot just rent a helicopter and fly to the heart of the matter without any inconvenience. We do not have the money to buy such a fantastic machine. So what shall we do? The obvious thing to do is walk, just to walk on our own feet, just walk. We have to get into the countryside of this intimate natural beauty and walk. This is exactly what the first step of meditation is, going into our natural psychological situation without trying to find some fancy touristic vehicle. There is no point dreaming about trying to get some exotic landrover or fantastic helicopter. It is a very pleasant thing, to begin with, to just walk.

The Buddhist tradition brings us the discoveries of the great teachers who have gone through this process in the past. It recommends to us straightforward meditation techniques, such as *annapannasati*, identification with breathing, and certain types of mindfulness practices. These practices are valid for our actual psychological situation. They are not millionaire's games. We cannot afford to get into exotic visualizations, magical practices, conjuring tricks of any kind. These are rich man's games—fancy landrovers, helicopters and jets. We have to work with what resources we have, we have to begin small, in an ordinary and simple way. Our actual present situation of what we are is our steppingstone. And we start from a simple technique such as walking or breathing. This is by no means expensive. It is a natural thing. We can breathe and walk—we have to breathe anyway; we have to walk anyway. That seems to be the starting point of meditation.

The relationship of meditation in this sense to the skandhas is quite interesting. The more we get into the gross, undisguised basic elements of what we really are, the more we relate to the skandhas. We cannot relate with the skandhas with masks on or dressed up in commentaries. We can only relate with the skandhas as they are in their naked and rugged state. We are meditating in a way which emphasizes form and the eight types of consciousness because we are trying to bypass the ignoring aspect of ignorance, which is the fundamental pain or the fundamental duality. We are trying to relate with the available bodily situation of breathing or walking. Doing this is very direct and very natural. The pain and pleasure of feeling need not be involved in breathing and walking. Those activities are just a simple source of ultimate natural beauty. And as far as perception is concerned, breathing and walking do not have to involve us in comparative criteria or relative notions of any kind, in logic, or any mind games at all. It is just simply breathing, walking, identifying with the simple process of being. And on the level of samskara, breathing and walking do not require us to associate with any type of thoughts. We do not have to connect ourselves with this type of thought or that type of thought. Thoughts present all sorts of fascinating possibilities: "Why don't we try to get into this virtuous thought of patience? Why don't I get into this virtuous thought of nonviolence? Why don't I just get angry, carried away by passion? Why don't I get smug and stay comfortable in my ignorance?" In the simple meditation practice of just breathing and walking these temptations do not apply because they are not really precise. They do not really have the precision that meditation presents—the sharp and awake and absolute precise quality of dealing with the actual situation as it is. If we are relating with this, we do not need anything further.

So consideration of the five skandhas has brought us to the point where we understand there is nothing else to do but meditate. And this particular picture of human psychology in terms of the five skandhas seems to be the only picture there could be. It convinces us that the only thing to do is just deal with something immediate and fresh. Meditating is just like collecting fresh vegetables from one's home garden instead of going to the supermarket and buying packaged things. We just walk out into the garden and collect fresh vegetables and cook them. That seems to be an exact analogy for meditation. Any questions?

Question. It seems to me you are saying that meditation for use at this stage of the game should be basic, at the kitchen-sink level, which would mean more bodily. I wonder if more subtle activities like talking or reading can be seen as basic bodily practices too.

Rinpoche. I think so, because you have to use your body. You have to read with your eyes; you have to hold your book in your hands, talking, you have to use your mouth.

Question. But then isn't awareness of the hands holding the book or the mouth making the words being unfair to the author or the person you are talking with? Isn't that overly self-centered?

Rinpoche. Well it depends on whether you are completely one with what you are doing or whether you are playing games. It is quite simple.

Question. You mention meditation as being a way of making friends with oneself; it seems to me more like making enemies with oneself, in that it seems to be a more painful process than the usual process of making friends. I wonder if you could clarify that a little bit.

Rinpoche. That painful experience is very good because that is the beginning of making friends with yourself. If you are really going to make a long-term friendship with somebody, probably the first thing that hits you about that person are the things that you do not like. That is the starting point that provides a foundation for your friendship. It is a really solid foundation, because having included those things you will not be perturbed later by whatever may happen with that friend. Since you know all the negative aspects and do not have to hide from that side of the relationship, you are now completely open to find the other side, the positive side, as well. That is a very good way to start making friends with oneself or anybody else for that matter. Otherwise you feel cheated when you discover the faults later on.

Question. How do the five skandhas tie in with meditation?

Rinpoche. That's a big question. The five skandhas are a process of five stages of psychological development and meditation does not contain that development. Meditation is just dealing with the situation that exists before the development took place or just continuing to deal with that basic situation while this development is taking place. In other words, meditation means getting simple rather than getting involved with the five stages. These five stages become insignificant or just purely external. That means that you are getting to the basic quality of the five skandhas rather than trying to follow their implications as we ordinarily do in a sort of hunting process, as though we are going to reach some valuable conclusion. It is getting to the basic point of the process without getting involved in the sidetracks.

Still, of course, the discovery of five types of processes there already is kind of very amusing. Although you are concerned with the basic point, the presence of the five processes helps keep you smiling.

Question. In the play between ignorance and intelligence that runs through the whole development of the skandhas there seem to be moments where the skandhas are not occurring. There seems to be a very rapid buildup and then, *poof,* the process goes away. And then it starts again.

Rinpoche. That is the whole point, there is a buildup and then this whole building-up process turns to dust. There is a gap, a space. And then either you build up again or you do not. But that kind of moment does happen. Automatically the process builds up; but before and after that, there is some space. It is like moving fast in one direction and having to turn and come back—you have to stop at the peak point. There is a moment of stillness; in the process of regenerating the speed, you have to stop at one point. That happens.

Question. Does one pass backwards through the skandhas? I mean if you were to sit down and meditate, first of all your mind would be full of thoughts. Then you meditate for a while longer and maybe your thoughts are not so discursively connected anymore so that then you relate directly to your perceptions. And then you reach a point where you are not so much relating to your perceptions anymore, they are not that important to you anymore. So then you feel just a vague sense of contact with your stream of associations. And then you have just a vague sense of sitting there. And then maybe you're in a nondualistic state. Could something like that happen?

Rinpoche. It sounds a bit fishy. You see, what you are talking about is going deeper and deeper, slower and slower. Somehow meditation does not happen that way. Once you go into the profundity, deeper and deeper and slower and slower, there is a possibility of being hypnotized by it so that you lose all contact with anything. You lose the dynamic quality of samskara, the dynamic quality of perception, the dynamic quality of feeling. And these are the only guidelines for buddha activity in a state of enlightenment. You do not want to push those out at all. You do not have go into a process of going deeper. Rather, at the beginning when you are dealing with form, a certain funny thing goes on between awakeness and confusion. There is a certain funny moment. That is where you strike first, whether you are using the breathing or the walking. Whatever your technique may be, that is your starting point. And meditation happens *right there*. You do not have to go through a process at all. The process just happens by itself. But the important point is the precision and sudden quality of that flash, a kind of first questioning created between sanity and insanity. That first moment of black and white, dullness and sharpness, is the starting point from where you relate with your breathing or your walking. You do not have to slow down at all. Meditation has nothing to do with working with the metabolism of the ego in that sense.

Question. In the Heart Sutra it says that Avalokiteshvara saw that the five skandhas were empty. Is that emptiness the same as the space you have just been talking about?

Rinpoche. Yes. The idea is—just flash. That is why it is important for a person to be free from his meditation as a concept, free from the idea "I am going to meditate," the sense of a ritual of any kind.

You see if a person is able to relate with his practice of meditation directly and simply on an everyday level, a sane level, then there is a possibility of perceiving the five skandhas as empty. Otherwise once you take the wrong starting point of working on the skandhas one by one systematically, then the five skandhas develop a system as well.

Question. Would the experience of emptiness be no less an aerial view than to see the minute workings of a situation, than seeing what is arising from moment to moment?

Rinpoche. Once you have a good aerial photograph of the whole area, that means that you have all the details in it as well. It is the same thing. Otherwise it cannot be called an aerial view. It is just a blurry picture.

CONSCIOUSNESS

THE FIFTH SKANDHA IS CONSCIOUSNESS. This involves a certain amount of explanation, since we already used the word "consciousness" at the beginning of the seminar in relation to the skandha of form as containing the eight types of consciousness. The consciousness of the fifth skandha is different from what we talked about before. Consciousness in the sense of the fifth skandha contains the final details of the process of the skandhas, the subtle fulfillment of the process. Consciousness in the first skandha is a sort of basic psychological background where the potentials of consciousness are present as eight types. Here, with the fifth skandha, we are talking about the fruition of those potentials. This is also described as eight types of consciousness, exactly the same categories in the same pattern as in the first skandha.

Another point that needs to be made clear here is the distinction between "mind" and "consciousness." In the Buddhist tradition, mind is purely that which perceives. It does not require brainwork; it is simple perception, just on the level of the nervous system. This simple instinctive function is called "mind." The Sanskrit term is *citta*, which literally means "heart," but it also means "essence," that basic essence of mind which contains the faculty of perception. This kind of perception called mind— reacting to hot and cold, favorable and unfavorable and so on—is very direct, simple and subtle at the same time. Consciousness, on the other hand, is articulated and intelligent. It is the finally developed state of being that contains all the previous elements. It contains all of the fundamental subtleties of "mind," the instinctive aspects on the level of feeling and it also includes thought patterns. It includes any kind of thinking process. But here the thinking process is on a subconscious level, whether it be discursive, pictorial or instinctive. Consciousness is that sort of fundamental creepy quality that runs behind the actual living thoughts, behind the samskaras. The explicit thoughts, the samskaras, are the actual grown-up thoughts, so to speak; whereas the thoughts produced by consciousness are the undergrowth of those thoughts. They act as a kind of padding. The whole pattern of psychology works in such a way that it is impossible for the explicit thoughts—virtuous thoughts or evil thoughts or neutral ones—to be suspended in nowhere, without any context whatsoever. The subconscious thoughts make the context that is necessary for the explicit ones. They constitute the sort of padding or background texture which permits the process to function in such a way that the next appropriate thoughts in the explicit sequence can come through. They are in a sense a kind of kindling.

So, you see, the whole pattern is now very efficiently set up. Now even if the second skandha of feeling does not operate quite completely, or if perception does not function quite properly, consciousness with its subconscious gossip can supply the missing element and keep the whole process in action. It acts as sort of an ignition. It starts up on a particular theme and then sends its message back to the other skandhas so as to activate the skandhic process, to get the whole mechanism going.

So consciousness constitutes an immediately available source of occupation for the momentum of the skandhas to feed on. And, as we discussed before, meditation provides almost the only occasion for that momentum to stop. That is exactly where meditation plays its very important role. Meditation provides some gap in the movement of samskara-type thoughts and even in the fabric of consciousness-type thoughts. It provides a gap which contains no kindling twigs. That gap creates a sort of chaos in the psychological process, chaos in the mechanism of building up karmic situations. That chaos helps to see what is underneath all these thought patterns, both of the explicit and subconscious types. It begins to reveal what is underneath.

What is underneath may not necessarily be particularly appealing. We might theorize that, according to the Buddhist teachings, what ought to be underneath is, of course, enlightened mind. But that is not quite so. At this point what is underneath is the collection of hidden suppressed thoughts. This layer is like the cloudy mind we talked about earlier on, but this time on the fifth skandha level. This is another bank of collected memories that have been placed there. Any kind of thing that you wanted to ignore, did not want to encourage or are ashamed of yourself about is put into this bank of confusion—the cloudy mind. The cloudy mind acts as a container for these collections. Ashamed thoughts, irrelevant thoughts, all sorts of unwanted material has been put aside there. And meditation provides the situation which brings these thoughts up because meditation goes right through the thought pattern and touches the ground of cloudy mind. In this way the bank is broken open, the container is broken open.

Because of this the probability is that the beginning practitioner of meditation will have to go through all sorts of emotional and aggressive thoughts. Particularly those thoughts that one does not want to see or hear any more come first. In meditation, consciousness acts as a starting point. One cannot meditate without consciousness. At the beginning one has to practice meditation purely on a thought level, a daydream level. It is only a pretense of meditation; one is pretending to meditate. But consciousness is being transformed by this pretense, by the suggestion that you are practicing meditation. In this way, the subconscious network, as well as consciousness itself, is gradually broken through. The speed of consciousness itself is slowed down and then one gets through to underneath.

So consciousness in the sense of the fifth skandha can be said to have two aspects—the subconscious aspect and the active aspect of the six senses and cloudy mind in action. This actualized functioning of cloudy mind is on another level altogether from the cloudy mind of the first skandha which was purely embryonic.

Maybe we should have discussion.

Question. Where does memory come in? Is it inherent in all the skandhas?

Rinpoche. Memory is connected with putting things into the cloudy mind. It is an active process in which consciousness picks certain themes and classifies them into particular connections and then sends that over to the cloudy mind, puts it in the bank of cloud mind along with the collection of wanted and unwanted thoughts that already exists there. What is in the cloudy mind is not only thoughts you dislike and have suppressed, but also content that you would like to play back again in the future for whatever purposes. It could be technical information, experiential material, pain and pleasure, hysterical things. Whatever it is, it is picked up by consciousness and put into that bank of cloudy mind.

Question. Why does it have to be "cloudy" mind? Why can't it just be mind?

Rinpoche. It is just mind, but mind cannot survive without relating to something, without relating that to this. Mind does not mean anything if there is no context of relativity. So that context of relativity which must be maintained in order to survive, that process of maintaining its consistent pattern *is* uncertainty, *is* confusion. The process of maintaining a sense of relativity is what confusion is. Because in order to keep something for future purposes or in order to hide from seeing it, we have to put it into a no man's land, an unresolved space. We have to put it away from the current focus of clarity. That *is* the cloudy mind, which does not have particularly sharp delineations of this in relation to that, but is just generally confusion.

Question. What is it that does the sorting, that suppresses things so that they get into the suppressed collection?

Rinpoche. It seems that consciousness picks out something and then hands it over to samskara and then that sends it to perceptions and feelings and then it is processed through and finally sent back to the bank. Consciousness sort of works like chopsticks. It picks an impression up and passes it to where it can begin to be chewed. It is not quite enough just to pick it up, it has to be refined in a sense, it has to pass through the process of all the skandhas.

Question. In meditating you pick up a thought, a disturbing thought, out of this cloudy bank. What happens then to the thought? Does it go back to the bank? Does it burn out? Does it ever disappear? Does it ever resolve itself?

Rinpoche. In many cases thoughts do not become resolved because the impression of a thought that you picked out still remains in the cloudy mind, a sort of reproduction of it remains there. In some cases, for instance during meditation, if we relate to thoughts as insignificant, that is, if we do not put them into categories of any kind, then they are not transferred back through the skandhas any more. They are not put back through the process, so they are suspended on the level of consciousness and are finally resolved. That is the way of resolving thoughts—through complete nonevaluation. As long as there is nonevaluation, the skandhas have no function. They do not know what to do with a nonevaluated thought because their language is the language of duality and evaluation. That is why they keep thoughts in a *bank*.

77

Question. So the job at hand would be to wipe out the cloudy mind through a kind of objectivity?

Rinpoche. Well, that is an extremely long process. Eventually the bank will wear itself out; but in the meantime we must keep on collecting as well.

Question. It sounds like duality has its own built-in pattern that ego is only part of. In other words, from what you're saying, it is not that the ego is selecting and fortifying only on its own behalf, but it seems that that kind of selection and fortification is inherent in the nature of duality itself. It is as though the skandhas just automatically select and sort like that without any particular interest.

Rinpoche. Yes, they are sort of slaves rather than intelligent. They have been given their job in accordance with their nature and they just react accordingly.

Question. Is there any way of working with the cloud mind other than meditation?

Rinpoche. There does not seem to be any other way at all. In order to get free of the pattern of cloudy mind we have to create chaos in the efficient mechanism of consciousness, and nothing can do that except absolute nothing—which is meditation. That seems to be the only way.

Question. Is it good to try to take some kind of positive step in working with your state of mind during meditation?

Rinpoche. You see, meditation should not be regarded as a learning process. It should be regarded as an experiencing process. You should not try to learn from meditation, but try to feel it. Any tendency to categorize what goes on during meditation as learning is an obstacle to meditation. This also applies to exotic techniques. They are also an obstacle because, when you use a technique which has an exotic flavor, you are more conscious of the technique than its application. So any technique used in the practice of meditation should be a purely functional one with no implication of any kind to it at all.

Question. How about reflection upon the nature of one's mind, or rather just sort of recognition of it?

Rinpoche. That is rather like contemplation in the sense of dwelling on something and going over it again and again. That means you have the subject you are working on and yourself separate. It becomes a sort of private show. You end up relating this to that, yourself to the subject matter. But meditation is an act of nonduality. The technique you are using should not be separate from you; it is you, you are the technique. Meditator and meditation are one. There is no relationship involved.

The trouble with contemplative practice is that there is always a relationship involved, some kind of criterion. Somehow this does not really cut the basic root of neurosis. The root of neurosis is conflict; neurosis requires the conflict of not knowing who you are, of not knowing what you are doing or how you relate with things. Neurosis needs to play this game of conflict. Therefore as long as some kind of resource for playing the game is provided, such as some subject matter, as long as some pretext is provided, you will go on and on with the game. Whether you do it in a genteel spiritual fashion or an ordinary fashion really does not matter. It is still a game.

Question. In the arts, there are techniques that one learns for the purpose of overcoming techniques, in order to be able to get to the direct experience part of it. I was wondering if, besides meditation, there are any other techniques that you could speak of that could help one in this way, some means to open oneself or to get closer to being.

Rinpoche. In addition to the sitting form of meditation there is the meditation practice in everyday life of panoramic awareness. This particular kind of practice is connected with identifying with the activities one is involved in. This awareness practice could apply to artwork or any other activity. It requires confidence. Any kind of activity that requires discipline also requires confidence. You cannot have discipline without confidence, otherwise it becomes a sort of torturing process. If you have confidence in what you are doing, then you have real communication with the things you are using, with the material you are using. Working that way, a person is not concerned with producing masterpieces. He is just involved with the things that he is doing. Somehow the idea of a masterpiece is irrelevant. The masterpiece, the perfect work of art, comes as a by-product of this process of identifying with what you are doing. You should not be too much concerned with producing a masterpiece.

Question. I'm confused about mindfulness and awareness. Is it that in doing everyday things, simple things, you practice mindfulness? And at the point where you forget what you are doing and go off into daydreaming, is that the point where you should start practicing awareness?

Rinpoche. In mindfulness practice there is very definite precision; every move, every minute detail is noticed. In the case of awareness practice you have the general outline of what you are doing, which covers the details as well, naturally. In practicing awareness in everyday life, at a certain point the wandering mind itself, the daydreaming mind itself, turns itself into awareness and reminds you. If you are completely one with the idea of awareness as being intimate, it is a true practice. That is, as long as your relationship to the idea of awareness is a very simple one and as long as your awareness practice is connected with sitting practice. In a proper practice of awareness, the complete proper relationship is that awareness comes towards you rather than you going towards it. In other words, if awareness is not possessed or owned, then it happens. Whereas if you try to possess and own awareness, if you relate to it as "my awareness," then it runs away from you. In order to understand this, you need to have the actual experience of it, rather than just reading the menu.

Question. I am very involved with music and for me art can only have a sense if it makes a complete statement of a certain very clear quality. In this connection I have been very much struck by the quality that emanates from certain ceramic lohans that can be seen in Western museums. I would like to find a way to begin to approach a statement of that sort in my own life. Everything else seems so trivial.

Rinpoche. Generally, the whole idea of appreciation is based, of course, on true understanding of things as they are. This means that you have to develop true understanding, which means understanding without other ideas put on it. If it is overlaid with other ideas, it becomes commentary or interpretation, rather than true understanding. True understanding is direct and simple appreciation, simple understanding without any criteria attached to it. I think this idea is expressed very clearly in a lot of Japanese art— flower arrangement, for example. Just a simple twig is chosen and just a couple of flowers are arranged in a certain way and the two elements are put together. Maybe there is a small rock beside them and a very simple plain background without any fancy designs behind, against which you can see the actual arrangement of flowers properly. The lohan that you mentioned also has that same simple quality. He just does not have any pretense of any kind. He just sits there. It reminds one of the Zen saying, "When I eat, I eat; when I sleep, I sleep." It is the same sort of thing.

When you sit, you sit properly. Just sit ordinarily. In fact the special quality of the lohan comes from the fact that he is so insignificant, absolutely insignificant; so ordinary that he is super-ordinary. It is because of that total ordinariness that he becomes special and radiates.

Question. Rinpoche, how does insanity fit in with the five skandhas? How would you explain insanity in terms of that system?

Rinpoche. Well, there seem to be two types of insanity—I do not know if insanity is the right word or not—two types of unbalanced states of mind. One of them is what we call "flipped," really mad. Because the world has come to appear totally and powerfully uncompassionate to the mad person, he sees every new event in terms of this total distortion and he loses his natural logic. This is connected with the distortion of consciousness, the fifth skandha. It is complete distortion on this level; on this level all criteria are lost. He is completely mad. His language is incoherent and he does all sorts of things that do not have any coherent significance. The other type is not mad at all in this sense. This type of person functions naturally, normally, looks after himself or herself, but distance is always being distorted. This sense of distance is the basic requirement for skillful communication. To communicate skillfully a person must be aware of interpersonal distance—a sense of whether he should reach out or whether he should wait. That kind of distance becomes very distorted so that communication is handled unskillfully; and there is frustration about that blindness. This brings on aggression and the demand for pain. This type is the egocentric, the egomaniac. Its main characteristic is the basic confusion of losing the sense of distance and this is connected with cloudy mind on the primeval level, as the background of all the skandhas. The confusion here is at the level where the original criteria separating this from that developed, at the level of the first development of duality. That is where distance first develops, the distance between me and that,

that and me. Because one becomes completely overwhelmed, involved, self-centered into so much *here*, one loses the distance. That is the extreme of egocentricity.

Question. Is that accessible to cure?

Rinpoche. I think both types can definitely be cured. But you see it is really tricky to cure problems like that. It depends very much on what sort of method you use. There are a number of methods which are seemingly good, but it turns out that the method itself can be turned into fuel. The process of cure itself becomes fuel for the disorder to live on. Somehow, the analysis method and the encounter-group-type method do not seem to be particularly the way. If you put a person in an encounter group, at the beginning the person might see things and do things completely honestly, in an open way; but then at a certain point the person begins to pick up the style of the other people taking part in the group and it becomes another kind of language. Quite probably, the person picks up a whole new style just for his participation in encounter groups. Very frighteningly, it becomes the ultimate kind of deception: the person is expressing everything, saying everything out, but at the same time there is a basic deception which is never expressed at all.

There is a certain danger in any purely analytic method. Somehow the word does not help very much at all. The word is actually the source of the confusion anyway. People who are "flipped" have a very skillful way of using words in accordance with their mad perspective; so the survival of their madness could be endless.

It seems that setting up a certain kind of general situation for the person is more effective. One starts with the basic physical situation of food and living environment. The whole idea of using the situation is to communicate with the unbalanced person so as to awaken him, so you start on the basic level of survival, the instinctive level, the level of the animal realm. The person should have some feeling of instinctive simple communication. Start that way. Then having established that kind of simple communication on the level of survival the rest becomes much easier and quite obvious.

Question. When these five skandhas are going along mechanically, just doing what they do, what happens when the individual who is part of these five skandhas becomes compassionate? What happens to the skandhas? Can you describe the process of compassion in terms of the skandhas?

Rinpoche. The basic idea of compassion is communication, skillful communication. That kind of skillful communication develops through relationships. This begins on the consciousness level. But in fact compassion is the source of transmutation of all the skandhas into the five tathagathas, or five aspects of enlightenment, that we discussed earlier. Compassion makes the skandhas function independently rather than as part of a chain. Ordinarily, feeling is dependent on form, form is dependent on feeling, feeling is dependent on perception and samskara and so on. They are all interdependent. They cannot be separate things. Whereas when the skandhas are transmuted into tathagatha principles, they become independent. In other words, all the skandhas have their independent mind and intelligence. This process of the skandhas becoming independent of each other begins from compassion. Communication based on this state of mind is the ultimate communication.

Question. I keep seeing the skandhas as part of the psychology of an individual. I see the process of compassion as someone behaving mechanically and then suddenly becoming sensitive. I'm still forced to see it somehow as a dualistic relationship, even when the five skandhas become five tathagathas. I mean the relationship of, say, a compassionate individual to those with whom he is relating.

Rinpoche. It has to remain a dualistic relationship still. Nothing is wrong with that at all. But in the case of compassion the process does not become centralized. You see, duality in the ultimate sense consists of wisdom and compassion; the two poles are necessary. If your five skandhas develop into the five tathagatha principles, you still have duality, but you are not baffled by it at all. It is a natural function. When we talk about nonduality we mean it in contrast to the bewilderment by duality that is the ordinary case.

Question. So the process of meditation is trying to cut the link between the skandhas? And a man who has done enough meditation, let us say, would have all the skandhas but they just would not be connected?

Rinpoche. Would not be connected, that is right. That is what is meant by cutting the karmic chain. The chain of karma is the five skandhas. And even after the links have been cut, the skandhas continue running, the process keeps running through. Actually the skandhas are not really linked; it is more that they are pushed one against the other. By meditating you are slowing down the process. When it has slowed down, the skandhas are no longer pushed against one another. There is space there, already there.

Question. When the five skandhas are functioning independently, what happens to memory?

Rinpoche. Memory becomes a sort of inspiration to each of them in their skillful activity. There is skillful activity because you do not have to refer back to memory any more. You see, memory is a very cowardly way of dealing with a situation. Since you are not in direct contact with the present situation, you have to refer back to what used to be. And you work that way. Whereas if you are relating directly to the present situation, as is the case with inspiration, then you do not require memory to work your way through the situation. You can tell everything from the present situation. Still you have the information of the past because of the present situation; in terms of the present situation rather than purely in the form of what was.

Question. In working on separating the skandhas, are they pushed apart one at a time, slowly, or does it happen suddenly all at once?

Rinpoche. It is extremely gradual process, like a wound healing. On the whole, there does not seem to be such a thing as sudden enlightenment as it is ordinarily understood. Of course there is sudden discovery of the different stages. This is like your discovering that your hair has gone gray, or that you have become fat.

Question. You have said that we begin to meditate with ambition. The consciousness is still in control of everything. And at some point, you said the bank of subconscious thoughts comes up and consciousness is no longer in control. This seems to me to be on the way towards enlightenment. What I wonder is, until we are enlightened, do we always meditate with ambition?

Rinpoche. You begin with ambition of some kind. Then at a certain stage meditation becomes instinctive. Then you cannot not meditate—it happens to you.

Question. But when the process of the skandhas starts reversing itself and consciousness is losing control, you have lost your original incentive. What you are doing no longer makes sense from the point of view you started from.

Rinpoche. Exactly, yes. That is the point at which the techniques begin to drop away; as well as any of the games that are involved in pretending to yourself that you are meditating.

Question. Well, during the gradual process that still goes on, what is it that becomes attractive about meditation, that replaces the ambition? People still want to sit down and meditate even if they are almost enlightened.

Rinpoche. You start with ambition and then meditation begins to seep into your system, so to speak. Gradually your system begins to require meditation. It is sort of an addiction, sort of an infiltration of your system begins to happen. That is what happens with bodhisattvas. They take a vow not to attain enlightenment, but they find one day that they have attained enlightenment anyhow because the practice has thoroughly infiltrated their system. Their behavior has become the complete embodiment of the dharma.

Question. In getting beyond duality, beyond criteria, there is still relativity and still form. There is still some kind of distinction between this and that. Wouldn't there then still be preference, say, for bliss, understanding, clarity? Or does it get to the point where it no longer makes any difference whether the forms are heavenly or domonic?

Rinpoche. There is a stage at which all of these sort of heavy-handed dualities dissolve. There is a very, very heavy-handed and solid duality in which without that, this cannot survive; because of this, that happens to be. You reach the stage of losing this sort of concept. And then you are conscious that you have lost that, got beyond it: you feel freer but at the same time you feel that you have gained something. But this is not quite final. You still have the memory that you have relinquished that heavy duality, that you used to have such ideas but you have lost them now. But a person gets beyond even that. One reaches a point where even the sense of the absence of duality no longer applies. The whole thing becomes very natural and obvious. On that level, a person really begins to perceive things as they are. A sort of transparent experience of duality begins to develop in which things are really precise without depending on each other. There is no sense of comparison, just precision. Black is black and white is white.

Question. I'm a little confused about the distinction between panoramic awareness which does not have the definite quality of mindfulness, and a kind of blurry state which comes up. I'm talking about the kind of blurry state in which one leaves tools all around, leaves one thing half finished to start another, etc. That seems to be the kind of dreamy state that frequently comes up just after one has finished meditation. It just does not seem to matter where you put your tools. Is panoramic awareness that kind of a blurry thing?

Rinpoche. The panoramic awareness of meditation in action contains textures. Texture are part of its scope. You see things in the right shape, in their own right shape, their own right situation— which is a kind of precision, sharpness. That sharpness and precision comes from experiencing the distance, proper distance, that we were talking about earlier on. You feel immediately the right skillful and active relationship with things or people. You experience them as they are, completely—so the tools belong to the toolshed. They are not knives and forks or anything else. You would not use the toilet to bathe and the basin to defecate. A sense of the proper relationship of things is included in your panoramic vision. You just would not do things the wrong way around. In the case of the blurry state, this is cloudy mind on the instinctive level. One is so much wrapped up in oneself that there is no chance for panoramic vision at all. There is nothing to be panoramic about. One is totally wrapped up in one's own little world. Others see you moving very slowly, very gently, saying very little, doing very mysterious things—but still that could hardly be described as a contemplative state of mind. It is more what has been described in the scriptures as a drunken elephant.

AUSPICIOUS COINCIDENCE

W E HAVE RUN OUT of scheduled subjects to talk about, and that in itself might be an interesting point to work on. The idea that applies here is what is known in Tibetan as *tendrel* [brten 'brel]. *Tendrel* literally means "coincidence" or "chance." This is something which very much underlies the functioning of the psychological movements described in the abhidharma. *Tendrel* is also the Tibetan translation of the Sanskrit *nidana*. The twelve nidanas are the twelve conditions in the chain reaction process of causation. The nidanas, like the skandhas, begin from ignorance and include feeling, perception, samskara, consciousness, name and form, sense perception, touch or contact, feeling, craving, grasping, intercourse, birth, old age and death.

The process of coincidence, the coming together of situations that happens through the nidanas, can be described as auspicious. We are familiar with the idea of an "auspicious occasion." Such and such thing happened, such and such people met, and all this combined so that such and such a fortunate event took place. This idea of auspiciousness is usually either regarded as just a form of speech or associated with superstition. It involves a sense of power. The word for "auspicious" as it relates with this notion of "coincidence" or *tendrel* is, in Tibetan, *tashi* [bkra.shis]; in Sanskrit, *mangalam*. Auspiciousness is an aspect of coincidence, of this meeting together of conditions. The movement of ignorance and feelings and perceptions, and so on, is an auspicious one, in a sense, an appropriate one; because all of these twelve causal links are related to each other continuously, infallibly. In other words,

91

there is no mistake about what is happening. Everything is right and appropriate at that very moment. That is what *mangalam* is, or *tashi*—a blessing. The Tibetan word *tashi* is composed of *ta* which means bright and *shi* which means fitting or good, appropriate. So it means "precisely fitting to the situation."

An example of this is our being here together. We all took a chance coming here. Nobody knew what this particular seminar was going to turn out to be like, but everybody did take that chance, made that commitment, and here we are. All the necessary conditions came together.

From this point of view, confusion, wandering in the samsaric realm of pain and misery, is not a punishment, not a mistake, but it is fitting, appropriate. It is an absolutely ideal situation. Of course, we could come to this conclusion by a kind of indirect reasoning based on a long-term view, saying that because of the samsaric situation we have an opportunity to study nirvana and liberation: without samsara there would be no nirvana, therefore samsara is an ideal situation. But our thinking need not take this long way around. If we really look directly, fundamentally, we can say that we need not have either samsara or nirvana. That is quite true. We need not have either. The whole situation need not exist. But it happens to be the case; so it is fitting.

This is not particularly an attitude of optimism. It is an attitude of pessimism and optimism together: the situation is fitting in that it is right and it is fitting in that it is wrong, both at the same time. The two poles are constantly present. "Right" is in its own way a healthy situation because it happens to be there. And "wrong" is also, in its own way, a healthy situation because it happens to be there. So the quality of *tendrel* and *tashi*, coincidence and auspiciousness, is inseparable from the karmic structure, the impetus that develops through the five skandhas and the twelve nidanas, inseparable from that whole apparatus which brings us into a situation.

So what we are actually studying is the whole process of karmic development without particular reference to which developments are the good ones and which are the bad ones. We are just studying the karmic situation as it is. It is fitting; all aspects of the process coincide in their particular unique ways in each and all situations.

This does not mean that everything is prearranged, that you have no choice at all—because everything happens in the present moment. Buddhist philosophy says that the future is vacant rather than prearranged. You cannot have a prearranged future; "future" means nothing has happened yet. Everything, as far as it exists, is in the present situation. The potential of the future is in the present moment. Therefore nothing can be prearranged or predestined. On the other hand, the whole thing is to a certain extent predestined because it is the past that presents us with the present situation. Predestination does go as far as that, to the present moment, and does not go beyond. Therefore there is room for the effort involved in the practice of meditation and in the commitment to spirituality to be important. That effort is helpful because it is a way of learning about the present situation and relating with it. If a person is able to meet the present situation, *tendrel,* the present coincidence, as it is, a person can develop tremendous confidence. He begins to see that no one is organizing the situation for him but that he can work for himself. He develops a tremendous feeling of spaciousness because the future is a completely open one.

This awareness of the auspiciousness of the karmic situation of the present moment is also to a certain extent a perception of the future. We may even perceive certain connections. But each case is an individual case. We can talk about having a karmic link with someone, but that link could not exist unless the two people involved were independent as well. Otherwise we could not speak of "link"; it would be one thing. Even if there is a link, it means that there are two independent people that have some connection with each other. So, even in that case, the whole process of this journey of involvement with the situation at that present moment is a lonely journey. Nobody can save you, help you. You yourself have to develop an appreciation and understanding of the process of chain reaction that happens. Looking at it in terms of the twelve nidanas is one way of seeing that.

There is the story of a certain arhat who is born into the particular karmic circumstances of a country without either teacher or teachings. As he grows up he develops questions about life. He takes long walks and at one point comes upon a charnel ground and finds an old piece of human bone. Picking it up and examining it, he questions where this bone comes from. The bone comes, obviously, from death. Where does death come from? Death comes from illness, old age. And he goes on in his reasoning, back and back—old age comes from birth and birth comes from intercourse and intercourse from feeling, touching, grasping and so on. He goes back, back, back. Finally he finds that the whole source and basic root is ignorance. He arrives at that conclusion just by looking at the bone and reasoning back. It is a kind of auspicious coincidence, a karmically auspicious chain reaction—you find a certain bone and you happen to sit down and look at it and think about it. This is an intellectual approach, it could be said, and also an intuitive one. It is not particularly extraordinary. Anyone could do it. Anyone could go back, step by step, finding some source for the previous conclusion, some obvious answer.

A lot of us are in a situation similar to that of this arhat—our present situation is that of having a certain dissatisfaction and wanting to find out more about it. A certain curiosity and dissatisfaction, curiosity and pain and pleasure and the knowledge that we have come across in our lives, have brought us here together. Having arrived at this point of being here, you question your result. Not only do you look back by way of an intellectual researching process, you also practice and experience what you are thinking about. Having experienced what you are thinking about, all life situations become much clearer, precise and obvious, at this present moment, right here.

So this concept of auspicious coincidence, *tendrel,* is extremely interesting and important. If a person realizes that a whole chain reaction of incidents brought him into the present situation, that solves a lot of problems. It means that you have already made a commitment to whatever you are doing and the only way to behave is to go ahead, rather than hesitating constantly in order to make further choices. It is like knowing that a certain restaurant serves a particular dish that you have in mind to eat; rather than wasting a lot of time reading the menu after you have sat down in the restaurant, go ahead and order that dish and eat it. In a sense it is a timesaving device to know that the incidents that happen in the round of life are constantly creating a particular unique situation. This is a very powerful insight which brings us a sense of freedom. It is knowing that at one and the same time you are not committed to the present situation and you are committed to it. But what we do with the present situation as it related to the future is completely up to us. It is an open situation.

This idea of chance or coincidence is fundamental to the abhidharma. What is described there has this character of taking place by coincidence, apparently by chance. This is a very important aspect of it. And it seems that today by chance we found our subject to talk about. Perhaps by chance we can have a discussion.

Question. As regards that open future you were talking about, I find that certain thoughts are constantly recurring in individuals. Everybody has their own style, their own thoughts, but it is as though a script for their whole life has been written. When they try to be completely blank with no conceptualization at all, certain thoughts in their own style keep flashing into their minds. Is this underlying gossip the fifth skandha? Is the continuity of this little gossip narrator going on all the time the person who is sort of writing the script of our lives? Whatever the case, that omnipresent script seems to keep the future closed rather than permitting it to be open.

95

Rinpoche. Strangely enough, actually, nobody writes the script at all. It just mysteriously happens. That is sort of a Zen answer rather than one in the style of methodical Indian philosophy. The abhidharma would say it differently. But I think it is a much clearer way of looking at this particular situation to say that nobody writes the script—it just happens. It is because there is nobody writing the script that so many varieties of things keep popping up. It is not that the thoughts happen particularly according to some logical pattern. Logically they might be quite dissociated; but things just pop up. They just happen out of nowhere.

Question. Is the fifth skandha the person that thinks he is writing the script? Making choices, giving coherence to your life?

Rinpoche. Once a thought pops up he has to acknowledge it. But he does not really dare to, really care to go back to the root of the thought. If he goes back to the root, he does not find any. He does not find anything at all.

Question. I still do not understand why certain kinds of thoughts keep recurring to certain people, no matter what they try to do. Even when they try to change, they look back and their pattern is still there. Where does everybody get their own style of thought pattern?

Rinpoche. Each person has his own style according to his type. There are different types of mentality—the mentality of aggression, the mentality of passion and all sorts of others. Different types of individuality originate from different types of basic energy. These are basic energies that misunderstood themselves, right at the beginning, and differentiated themselves from the basic ground. That basic ground is an open one but the energies it contains are colorful. There will be red with a tinge of yellow,

yellow with a tinge of green, white with a tinge of pink. The certain basic energies which also carry the tinge of a certain style of emphasis. For instance, there could be hatred which finds emphasis through passion; the basic quality is hatred but it develops in terms of passion. There could also be other combinations, such as a basic quality of pride with emphasis through ignorance. All sorts of combinations of sparks of light develop. Then they become individuals, detached from the main ground, like satellites. In this way, we each develop our particular version of ignorance, because of those particular colors, so to speak, that we had right from the beginning. Our particular individual style with its particular energies runs through all the processes of psychological evolution—the five skandhas, the twelve nidanas and so on. But this is not a hangup at all. It is our wealth. We each are a particular type of person with a particular type of mania; and that is good.

Question. Could you speak a little more about the commitment to the present situation you were talking about, and particularly how to distinguish that from the ego's commitment to extend itself?

Rinpoche. Somehow the ego's commitment to extend itself has no direction. The ego's movement is not a flowing one. It is simply trying to maintain its own house. Since ego's commitment involves purely this maintenance sort of mentality, there is really no sense of journey involved at all. In the case of the commitment to the present situation, there is a movement or journey. The sense of journey consists in the fact that, from the point of view of this commitment, every situation contains a unique drama.

Question. Are you saying that one no longer finds everything familiar?

Rinpoche. Situations need not be familiar. Ego's commitment tends to rely on a sense of familiarity or feeling that nothing is happening. A person might sit down to meditate and feel that nothing is happening even though he is extremely agitated. He has pain in his back, pain in his neck and flies are buzzing all around. He is extremely agitated and yet he feels that nothing is happening. But it is possible to experience every moment as having individuality in it. Once you are in a situation, you go along with the unique patterns of it, its particular textures and so on. This is quite different from ego's commitment to maintaining itself as a solid thing. Ego would find acknowledging the unique individuality of every situation extremely threatening. But relating that way to each situation as it is is a path. There is a great deal of movement in it. You are constantly facing a drama of some kind.

Question. But then there is no other direction than that of each situation?

Rinpoche. That is a much more definite kind of direction than having a map or blueprint to follow. It is a real direction. Pain will be real pain and pleasure will be real pleasure. Confusion will be real confusion. Every situation will be a true situation, a precise one—and that is the guidance, that is the pattern that you go along with. Looking back we find that all the situations in which we have had a sense of making a journey were situations of living constantly in the present moment. There was no sense of predestination involved at all. The present situation is the destination as well as the path.

Many people wish to secure their destination in the future now. But the future is not here yet, that is why it is the future. It is amazing the extent to which we deceive ourselves, stretching ourselves to all sorts of territories and situations that are purely imaginary. It is as though the whole future is planned and a planned time has been stretched all the way back from the present moment and all the way forward from the present moment. Then everything is overcrowded. Looking at things this way we manage to set ourselves into a great deal of paranoia and panic. But if one really sees the present situation as it is, it is always a quite simple one.

Question. Can you speak about when one is sitting in meditation and bodily discomforts arise and one is taken up by the feeling of discomfort and boredom? But then one oscillates from this to the commentary that the discomfort and so on is just something for one to cling onto as an entertainment. But then one clings to the commentary. And somehow there is nothing there in any of these moments which is free. There is only oscillation back and forth between these various clingings.

Rinpoche. It seems that the idea of the commentary and trying to make something out of it becomes self-destructive or confusing. There is an analogy used in the scriptures of discursive mind being like a silkworm. A silkworm has a web of its own substance around it. It survives by churning out more silk. You see, the situation is very simple. When bodily pain or pleasure arise it is very simple. You just perceive it and just leave it. You do not have to put it through any process of any kind. Each situation is unique. Therefore you just go along with it, let it happen according to its nature.

Question. I guess what I can't quite understand is what you mean by "go along with."

Rinpoche. It is a matter of acceptance. Even though the acceptance of what is happening may be confusing, just accept the given situation and do not try to make it into something else; do not try to make it into an educational process at all. Just see it, perceive it and then abandon it. If you experience something and then disown that experience, you provide a space between that knowledge and yourself which permits it simply to take its course. Disowning is like the yeast in the fermentation process. That process brews a state of mind in which you begin to learn and feel properly.

Question. Does it matter if the disowning is only another form of commentary in the beginning? Or is that inevitable?

Rinpoche. You cannot start from absolute, complete perfection. Being perfect does not matter. Just perceive and experience and disown. It does not matter how and what. The problem is that we always want to start something and at the same time make sure that what we are doing is right. But somehow we just cannot have that kind of insurance. One really has to take a chance and accept the raw and rugged quality of the situation. You could have a commentary-type situation where there is constant analysis involved. But that analysis is just part of the process. Just leave it that way. It does not have to become final. There is nothing the matter with your commentary as long as you do not try to take it as a final conclusion. You should not try to make it into a definite, recorded message with the idea of playing it back when you need it. Because when you play it back you will be in a different situation, so that it will automatically be out of date.

Question. In the moment when that commentary exists there is so much clinging to that commentary.

Rinpoche. The commentary without being given special value is okay. It is just chatter. That is okay. Let it be that way. You should not interfere with that energy that is going through.

Question. When a conflict arises I usually feel that I have control of the situation. I feel that I can make a choice. But now I am wondering whether I actually make a choice or not.

Rinpoche. There is nothing the matter with the idea of choice. In dealing with a situation, the choice is there already. The choice consists of two aspects of the situation that are happening at the same time; those two aspects provide a basis for your making a relationship with either of the alternatives. The way to work with that is, in making that choice, not to go according to your sense of comfort but go according to straightforwardness. If there are two choices, one is ahead of you, right in front of you, and the other choice is slightly off-center. There may be ten or twelve hundred choices, but there is one choice waiting for you on the road. The rest of them are waiting on the side, as sidetracks. Therefore the other choices waiting on the side become more attractive, like restaurants and drive-in movies on the side of the road. The choice has to be straightforward, based on common sense, basic sanity. Actually, it is transcendental common sense.

One could misunderstand what I have been saying. If I say that by going along with the present situation the future becomes quite clear, that could be misunderstood in the sense that everything is marked out for you. It could be misunderstood in the sense of there being divine guidance. You could think that everything has been prepared for you so you can immediately find your place, as in the saying, "The swan is in the lake and the vulture is in the graveyard." This is not quite the case. Relating with the present moment is quite difficult and painful in many cases. Although it is straightforward, a straight road, it is quite a painful one. It is like the bardo experience mentioned in the *Tibetan Book of the Dead.* You have a brilliant light coming at you with the image of a certain tathagatha peering at you from within it. And on the side there is a less brilliant, less irritating light. The light from the side is much more beautiful because it is less glaring, only a reflection of the tathagatha. So there are two choices. Should we go into the irritating one or should we just turn off on one of the sidetracks.

This symbolism from the *Tibetan Book of the Dead* is very profound for our actual, everyday life situation. It does not have to refer only to after-death experience. Perhaps the after-death experience just typifies the kind of situation in which choices are most enlightening or stimulating and most immediate. In our ordinary life situation we have to open ourselves and investigate and see and then make a commitment. Without choice, there would be no leap and no moment of letting go at all. Because of choice, therefore, there is a moment of leap and letting go happens. So it seems that it is not particularly comforting and blissful and easy. On the other hand it could be inspiring. That much at least could be said.

Question. You seem to be talking about the discovery of wisdom. Could you say more about that?

Rinpoche. The discovery of wisdom has nothing to do with the centralized quality of ego. It is not actually a discovery at all because *you* cannot see that you are discovering. You become part of wisdom. You transcend the transcendental knowledge of prajna and you reach to the level of the jnana, real wisdom. This is actually very disappointing because we would like to watch ourselves being enlightened. But that is impossible. That rewarding experience of confirmation, that finally you have made it, here you are, is impossible. That would never happen.

Question. When you make choices you don't seem to have to think about it, but something spontaneous leaps up and makes the choice before you think about it. Before you can choose something else makes the choice for you.

Rinpoche. It all depends on how much of a big deal you make out of the choice itself. If you do not make a big deal about the choice, you cannot be conned or seduced by anything on the sidetrack. By the time those seductions arise you are going on anyway. So you go ahead, you go straight.

Question. Is this straightforward choice the same as intuition?

Rinpoche. It is spacious intuition, intuition which is not based on the animal level of instinct. It is the kind of true intuition which is not connected with the survival of ego.

Question. In this context of making choices where does "crazy wisdom" come in?

Rinpoche. Crazy wisdom is the sort of basic impetus behind the whole process of working with the situation. In order to make a decision which is straightforward but not particularly pleasurable, one has to have some power behind one. That is the element of crazy wisdom, that basic power behind the situation. But this does not mean that you should just find the most painful alternative and make your decisions according to that. The tendency here does not have to be suicidal, masochistic. You would not get into that either.

Question. Again in relation to choice, I was thinking about the forms of divination that you mention in *Born in Tibet*. Is a technique of divination used in a situation where there is a vagueness about going straight ahead?

Rinpoche. Divination is generally used when you are somewhat trapped by the situation. You really have no alternative but you are too cowardly to commit yourself to your actual intuition of the straightforwardness. So you turn to the pretense of divination. And what happens in divination is that, even though you may be highly biased in your view of the situation, you pretend not to be. You step out of the situation altogether and then you open your mind and allow yourself to make a decision in accordance with the divination practice. Or, more precisely, once you are there in no man's land, the answer is there already. Then you come back to your own territory and make a decision.

Question. So it is not that divination has the answer, but rather it is a vehicle for stepping out?

Rinpoche. Yes. Divination is like a sword. So you take the step and you use it. You cut the doubt.

Question. I find a certain seductive and fascinating quality in getting into and submitting to the teaching. There is a feeling of something very strange and novel and open and one is pulled along quite willingly. But at the same time I am suspicious of the fascination aspect of it.

Rinpoche. We have to allow ourselves some steppingstones. It is not necessary to be so severe. You see, that is the wonderful thing about the four noble truths—they begin from *duhkha,* pain. They start from the bottom where the most important things are, rather than from the top where the most refined things are, the cream and all. It starts from the spices and minerals and everything that floats down to the bottom. You begin with the dirty work, but that in itself becomes a steppingstone. And then gradually, more and more, you discover the top layer. And since you discover it gradually it comes as no surprise. Whereas if one starts with the beautiful and rich things in the top layer, then one does not want to come down because there is the possibility of finding other things underneath. One does not want to associate with that. One begins to discover that there is something fishy. You do not want to go down to the bottom because you fear you will discover something unpleasant. So we begin from underneath, with the most gross part. That is our starting point. One does not have to start perfect or beautiful. Starting from the bottom, the whole structure is fundamentally sound. Since you have already dealt with the worst things, what could happen worse?

In our style of teaching, we could start from the cream. But then a person would not be satisfied with the cream because he has not been given any impression of the value of it. Therefore we have to go through the whole evaluation process. We have to start from the bottom and then come up. That could be called a useless game from the point of view of enlightenment itself, but from the point of view of the unpeeling, the unmasking process, it is necessary. It is a game, the practice is a game, but one has to go through it.

There is a story of a mother and child living together. And the child asks the mother, "Where is my father?" And the mother says, "He is a wonderful person, but you cannot find him." The child gets very curious about his father and the mother keeps telling him stories about how wonderful his father is. The child's expectations get more and more built up until finally the situation reaches a point where the mother has actually to take him to see the father. So the mother takes her son out the front door of the house and the two go up into the mountains. They climb steep slopes and cross streams and labor over all kinds of obstacles. Finally they reach a ridge from where they can look down. They look down and see a valley with a house in it. The mother says, "That house down there is where your father lives." Then they climb down to the house and enter at the back door. In the room, they find a man and the mother tells her son, "This is your father." After the tremendous effort of the journey, climbing and walking a long way, the child is tremendously excited and very pleased to find his wonderful father. Then the child discovers a door on the other side of the room that leads into the very same house where he had always lived with his mother. The mother could have taken her son directly through the door to see the father, but the child would not have appreciated him unless they had made this journey. If the mother just took the child from one room to the other, it would not have been anything.

PRACTICE & INTELLECT

I T SEEMS that in this seminar we have been able only to under-
take a simplified synopsis of abhidharma and to provide some
impression of the fundamental principles underlying the
abhidharma descriptions. To study abhidharma in detail would
require a lot more time. Still I think we have gotten an idea of the
general outlines of abhidharma as a sort of psychological map. I
think our exchange has been quite rich and I hope this seminar
will sow the seed of further study on this material.

The main thing that we have been trying to do is to make the
study of this particular subject experiential. Some attempt has
been made towards an approach that would permit a practitioner
to become a scholar and a scholar to become a practitioner. This
can be done if we work closely enough with our basic psychology
and with our basic process of intellectual understanding. So our
approach has been quite unique. No perfect scholar would study
this way and no perfect practitioner would look at the subject as
we have. On the other hand, an open scholar and an open practitioner might both find it quite appropriate.

Looking at abhidharma this way, nothing is terribly abstract. A
lot of the ideas might be abstract if isolated as ideas; but actually
they are not abstract because they have real bearing on our personal experience. The psychology of one's own being shows the
operation of the five skandhas and the whole pattern that they are
part of.

Most studies of abhidharma tend to regard the five skandhas as
separate entities. As we have seen, this is not the case; rather they

constitute an overall pattern of natural growth or evolution. This fact alone could bring a lot of understanding. Without seeing that the five are part of an overall pattern that has been clearly understood, one might want to ask, "Why five skandhas? Why not ten? Why not one?" If five was just a random number, if the basic approach was arbitrary, there would be no end to the collections and classifications that we could concoct. But the way of looking at abhidharma that we have attempted makes it possible to see that the idea of five stages is not just random. It makes it possible to see that there is a general pattern which has five fundamental aspects. Of course, it is not absolutely necessary to talk about five aspects in order to see that evolutionary pattern. The understanding of that pattern is also reflected in a number of other sets of classifications that we have not had a chance to discuss. The fundamental point of abhidharma is to see the overall psychological pattern rather than, necessarily, the five thises and the ten thats. This kind of primary insight can be achieved by combining the approaches of the scholar and the practitioner.

There is an immense wealth of teachings that, hopefully in the future, we will be able to study in this manner. It is not necessary to look at the subject matter in just a simpleminded, emotional way; nor in just a cold analytical way. Scholarship and direct insight can work together. Teaching in this way is, in a sense, more of a matter of stimulating interest than purely conveying information. And therefore it applies to students no matter what stage of sophistication they have achieved. That is why it is said, "The dharma is good at the beginning, the dharma is good in the middle and the dharma is good at the end." Each presentation of the dharma has its own unique qualities, for advanced students as well as beginners. One thing continues right through the stages, which is what is called "the secret doctrine." The secret teaching goes on throughout. Discussing abhidharma, somehow we have covered more than abhidharma. We have touched a great deal on some of the tantric possibilities involved in a further odyssey into the teaching. All this is what is known as "self-secret." There is no copyright and nothing is being hidden. Everything is presented, as much as could possibly be understood. But a great deal could be secret from the audience's point of view. If one is not ready to hear the advanced aspects of the subject, one hears it purely from a beginner's point of view. Whereas if one is ready to hear in a semigrown-up style, one hears in that way.

So the responsibility for understanding a seminar is not based solely on the speaker, nor solely on the audience. We manufacture it together. It is our child that we produce; it is our dance. And as the dance takes place, the music happens by itself. When things happen in this way, they have a living quality. This is not purely experimental. At the same time as being alive, there is something established and familiar about it. Even though exchange happens spontaneously, the subjects that arise in our talks and discussions are not arising for the first time. This has happened before many times over again. Generations and generations of people have thought this way and found out and understood this way, spontaneously, as we have. And the ideas have been handed down and presented. It is like a good baker handing down his knowledge of bakery. The knowledge is, in a sense, old, but each time the bread is baked, it is hot and fresh. There is no cold bread. Still there is that knowledge of bakery which is very established, even though the bread is baked on the spot. This can be very inspiring. Once one is committed to the teachings, this living and inspiring quality is there continuously.

We could have discussion.

Question. I am still not sure about the relation between practice and the intellect. Do we have to keep them separate or is there some way that we can use intellect in our practice?

Rinpoche. Let me tell you something about my own training. In Tibet we not only attended talks but also memorized the texts; every day we had to memorize about six pages. The following day someone would be chosen by lottery to present what he had heard

109

the day before, with the commentary and everything. And he would be asked questions about what he had heard the day before. There was no way of getting out of it. At the beginning it was quite a good discipline. But at a certain stage the whole thing became very monotonous. It felt like we were being programmed into this structure of scholarly learning. We couldn't hear things anymore; we just memorized the words. We could even discuss the subject from an intellectual point of view, but we didn't really understand it. We couldn't properly hear ourselves, let alone what other people were saying. Usually such a course would take about six months. We would learn the abhidharma text itself and the Indian commentary, and then the Tibetan commentary on that commentary. There were also various theses written on particular abhidharma subjects from the point of view of the Gelugpas, the Kagyüpas, the Sakyapas, the Nyingmapas and so on. So we would try to bring everything together. But it was just too much material. Somehow it had the hypnotic effect of hearing something over and over and over. The teachings echoed in our heads continuously; we even dreamt about it. When we would get up in the morning certain quotations would pop into our heads. Finally the six months course of study was finished. We were told that we had learned abhidharma but we thought we really had not heard anything. We were just happy to get rid of the whole thing so we could relax, go off for a summer holiday or something. But somehow we couldn't really take a complete vacation; the discipline kept coming back to us constantly. We realized afterwards that we were really involved with the teaching. Whatever we were doing, talking to people, walking in the mountains, riding a horse, or camping on the mountainside, abhidharma would come back constantly to haunt us like a ghost. Then we would begin to understand a few things, maybe just one or two ideas at the beginning, but as we got into it more and more we began to get curious about the whole thing. Just out of curiosity we would open the book and read a few little passages. And they began to mean something.

The point is that certain things may be out of your reach. But if you have the discipline to listen to them, at a certain moment they become appropriate to you. They come back to you automatically, by themselves, rather than by your attempt to really tune into them and work on them.

Question. What you just touched on is something I have not been clear about for a long time, namely, using a form of conditioning in the service of becoming free of conditioning. My thinking has been that all it does is just stuff one up with more material, whereas I am really interested in being free of conditioning.

Rinpoche. I suppose that's largely dependent on the type of conditioning involved. For instance the intense indoctrination taking place in China is very impressive at the moment because you can see what they have achieved by it. But as soon as you step out of China, the whole thing becomes irrelevant; the conditioning doesn't apply once you step out of that environment. Whereas certain ideas that do apply to you personally may not be particularly obvious at the time. But even if you step out of the learning situation, they are still applicable, even more so. In meditation practice you start by putting yourself into a conditioning process. But by doing that, the conditioning itself wears out. The process of conditioning begins to develop seeds, but the conditioning itself goes away. Then the seeds begin to ferment.

Question. Don't you get a little high on this fermentation?

Rinpoche. You always get high.

Question. What's the difference between having these ideas coming back to you in daily life and the kind of extraneous commentary you have characterized as the "spiritual advisor"?

Rinpoche. The idea of a spiritual advisor is more the pious attitude of trying to be good and spiritual all the time. Whereas in this case you have no idea of what you should be doing, you just go along doing your ordinary things. The ideas just pop up. Of course if you begin to hold onto them, it could turn into a spiritual advisor. We are talking about ideas breaking through spontaneously, which is quite different from the deliberate spiritual advisor of ego.

Question. Then should one's approach to the abhidharma scriptures be more like reading a novel rather than studying something so that you can use it in a particular way later? Should we approach it in a way which is more free of purpose, something like a chess game or a puzzle, and forget about trying to apply it to our meditation?

Rinpoche. Yes and no. You can go too far. Finally you may find that you are not reading at all, because not reading is more appealing or you are sick of the whole boring subject. You have to have some discipline of applying your mind to it. You should think in terms of how you could apply it to yourself. But if you become too ambitious, trying to digest every little detail, you can't do it.

The idea is to try to feel the general outline of the whole thing rather than being too faithful to every sentence, every word. That kind of attitude has become a big problem in the study of Buddhism. If you are too involved with details, you might lose the perspective as a whole. But if you are able to feel the whole pattern, the outline of the whole thing, you will find it much more applicable to your life. And once that has happened, the details begin to come up by themselves—spontaneously. For instance, if you have a basic understanding of the development of the five skandhas, you have a feeling for the whole process, so the details cease to become isolated, disconnected facts. Instead they are just part of that map.

Question. Is there a point, if you learn these things more or less by rote, where they become a part of your feelings and your conceptions?

Rinpoche. There seem to be two ways to approach it: the highly disciplined way of taking in everything without choice, or trying to work along with your interest. But, if you take the second approach, that interest should bear on the overall context, so that you don't get carried away by fascination for one particular aspect of the subject.

Question. Supposing that one is quite willing to give up any idea of choice and to take in anything that might eventually become a part of oneself.

Rinpoche. Well that suits one type of personality. It's the kind of conditioning process that we have been talking about, like meditation. Whether you like it or not, you go on meditating. It may not be particularly pleasurable, in fact it could be extremely boring. Memorizing or reading doesn't have to be directed only towards apparently profound or high-falutin subjects. It could be very ordinary and simple. From that simplicity you can learn a great deal. There was a tradition in Tibet that certain teachers were expert on particular short writings of various great teachers. Every year a camp was set up and these teachings were presented very simply. Hundreds of people attended these summer study groups although the same thing was said every year in exactly the same way. But each year they went a little bit further in their understanding. Not only the students but the teachers themselves found that each year it was as though they had never read those particular sentences before.

Question. When you said that the reading is to be applied to our meditation, you didn't mean thinking about it during meditation, did you?

Rinpoche. No, but by providing some sense of space and openness meditation is good preparation for reading. If you allow yourself some gap or space to rest by sitting down and doing absolutely nothing, you recover from your speed. Then you are in the right state of being to read and absorb more.

Question. When we first start noticing some of the things we have learned about in abhidharma in our own psychological processes, how can we see the interconnectedness of these processes and not just get hung up on identifying them: "Aha, I see this! It talks about it in the abhidharma."

Rinpoche. If you recognize something on the spot that way, it is automatically interconnected. That inspiration is based on the cause-and-effect pattern that is part of the whole. But I think the main point is that one shouldn't get carried away with pride about finding something in your being that matches the abhidharma. The point is not to fit things into some system or to prove anything to yourself, but to see the pattern as it is. You just recognize it and go on. It is not a big deal.

Question. I don't understand the time scale that the twelve nidanas happen on. Do they happen in each moment or does it take a whole lifetime or many lives?

Rinpoche. They take place every moment. The twelve types of chain reaction have to take place in order to bring daily experience into action. They form a pattern. They are not independent; each of them depends on the previous one as well as the next one. But that whole development could happen in one fraction of a second. The abhidharma compares the twelve nidanas to a stack of paper. You could put a needle through it in one second. If that process were divided so that you could consider the point at which the needle penetrated the first piece of paper, then the next, then the next, there would be twelve of them. And those twelve could be divided into three parts each—touching, penetrating, coming through and touching the next one. This process, which constitutes ego mind, can be divided endlessly, which is why ego as a solid thing does not exist. It cannot be found in any part of this process. Things happen very momentarily, and there is no solid independent thing such as me and mine.

Question. Does that mean that each moment is one of these cycles of twelve?

Rinpoche. Yes.

Question. Let's say I was able to see each step in the process—

Rinpoche. You wouldn't be able to see each step in the process. It would be impossible.

Question. What could you see?

Rinpoche. You could perceive the whole pattern, perceive it rather than see it. Regardless how sharp your mind was you couldn't see them as long as you regarded each of the twelve as separate.

Question. You mean you could perceive it by being part of it?

Rinpoche. Yes, you could be part of it, and you could feel it that way.

Question. What is the thread of continuity between those twelve steps?

Rinpoche. The process begins with ignorance and ends with death and then death produces ignorance again. It goes on and on.

Question. But there must be a thread of connection, otherwise there would be absolutely no continuity. I would see you one moment and the next moment I would be sitting in England seeing my mother.

Rinpoche. The body is the connection. The mind-body, rather than the physical body, that is, the central headquarters of ego. You report back to your mind-body, your nest. If you ask a person, "How do you know that you are what you are?" the only simple way of explaining it is because, "I see myself in the mirror. I am what I am. I have a body." But, if you try to go beyond that and find some further principle to base it on you would not find anything. That's why the Heart Sutra says "There is no eye, no ear, no nose, no tongue, no body. . . ." Your eye is just an eye, it's not your eye; your nose is a nose, but it's not your nose. Nobody is you. Through the whole system of your body, every part has its own name, its own place. It is made out of a lot of things, but there is no such thing as you.

So one begins to transcend the mind-body, one's version of the body as a solid thing, by seeing the individuality of each particle in the body. But you do not have to destroy the body. You learn through the body.

Question. So your teaching is to try to show us how to transcend our attachments, which constitute the mind-body.

Rinpoche. We are not exactly transcending the notion of a body altogether, but we are trying to step out of the tendency towards nesting in the body, that tremendous security notion we have that the body is a fortified place and that you can go back to your fort. Even if we get beyond that, continuity does not seem to be a big problem. We still have to have some basis for dealing with other people because, having got beyond ego, we develop compassion and a sense of compassionate communication. In order to communicate with other people there has to be somebody who is communicating, and that kind of continuity goes on. That has nothing to do with ego at all. Ego is imagination of a centralized nest that gives secure protection. You are frightened of the world outside of your projections so you just go back into your sitting room and make yourself comfortable.

There is a general misconception about Buddhism in relation to this point. People wonder who, if there is no ego, is attaining enlightenment, who is performing all one's actions? If you have no ego, how can you eat, how can you sleep? In that case ego is misunderstood to be the physical body, rather than what it is—a paranoid insurance policy, the fortified nest of ego. You being can continue without your being defensive about yourself. In fact you become more invincible if you are not defending yourself.

Well, this seems to be the end of this particular seminar on abhidharma. But it could be the beginning of our learning process. So we will end our seminar and our seminar will continue.

Shambhala Dragon Editions

The Art of War, by Sun Tzu. Translated by Thomas Cleary.

The Awakened One: A Life of the Buddha, by Sherab Chödzin Kohn.

The Awakening of Zen, by D. T. Suzuki.

Bodhisattva of Compassion: The Mystical Tradition of Kuan Yin, by John Blofeld.

The Book of Five Rings, by Miyamoto Musashi. Translated by Thomas Cleary.

The Buddhist I-Ching. Translated by Thomas Cleary.

The Compass of Zen, by Zen Master Seung Sahn. Foreword by Stephen Mitchell.

Cutting Through Spiritual Materialism, by Chögyam Trungpa.

Dakini Teachings: Padmasambhava's Oral Instructions to Lady Tsogyal, by Padmasambhava. Translated by Erik Pema Kunsang.

The Diamond Sutra and The Sutra of Hui-neng. Translated by A. F. Price & Wong Mou-lam. Forewords by W. Y. Evans-Wentz and Christmas Humphreys.

The Essence of Buddhism: An Introduction to Its Philosophy and Practice, by Traleg Kyabgon.

The Experience of Insight: A Simple and Direct Guide to Buddhist Meditation, by Joseph Goldstein.

A Flash of Lightning in the Dark of Night: A Guide to the Bodhisattva's Way of Life, by Tenzin Gyatso, the Fourteenth Dalai Lama.

Glimpses of Abhidharma, by Chögyam Trungpa.

Great Eastern Sun: The Wisdom of Shambhala, by Chögyam Trungpa.

Insight Meditation: The Practice of Freedom, by Joseph Goldstein.

Lieh-tzu: A Taoist Guide to Practical Living, by Eva Wong.

The Lotus-Born: The Life Story of Padmasambhava, by Yeshe Tsogyal. Translated by Erik Pema Kunsang.

Mastering the Art of War, by Zhuge Liang & Liu Ji. Translated and edited by Thomas Cleary.

The Mysticism of Sound and Music, by Hazrat Inayat Khan.

The Myth of Freedom and the Way of Meditation, by Chögyam Trungpa.

Nine-Headed Dragon River: Zen Journals 1969–1982, by Peter Matthiessen.

Returning to Silence: Zen Practice in Daily Life, by Dainin Katagiri. Foreword by Robert Thurman.

Rumi's World: The Life and Work of the Great Sufi Poet, by Annemarie Schimmel. [Summer 2001]

Shambhala: The Sacred Path of the Warrior, by Chögyam Trungpa.

The Shambhala Dictionary of Buddhism and Zen. Translated by Michael H. Kohn.

The Spiritual Teaching of Ramana Maharshi, by Ramana Maharshi. Foreword by C. G. Jung.

The Sutra of Hui-neng, Grand Master of Zen: With Hui-neng's Commentary on the Diamond Sutra. Translated by Thomas Cleary.

Tao Teh Ching, by Lao Tzu. Translated by John C. H. Wu.

Teachings of the Buddha, revised & expanded edition. Edited by Jack Kornfield.

Vitality, Energy, Spirit: A Taoist Sourcebook. Translated and edited by Thomas Cleary.

The Way of the Bodhisattva: A Translation of the Bodhicharyavatara. Translated by the Padmakara Translation Group.

Wen-tzu: Understanding the Mysteries, by Lao-tzu. Translated by Thomas Cleary.

Zen Essence: The Science of Freedom. Translated and edited by Thomas Cleary.